Life-Giving Spirit

Life-Giving Spirit

RESPONDING TO THE FEMININE IN GOD

Alwyn Marriage

First published in Great Britain 1989
SPCK
Holy Trinity Church
Marylebone Road
London NW1 4DU

231.2

British Library Cataloguing in Publication Data

Marriage, Alwyn
Life-giving spirit : responding to the feminine in God
1. Christian doctrine. God. Linguistic aspects
I. Title
231
ISBN 0 281 04430 9   26025950

Typeset by Deltatype Ltd, Ellesmere Port, Cheshire
Printed in Great Britain by
Biddles Ltd, Guildford and King's Lynn

*This book
is dedicated to
my human mother,
Alwyn Sherratt,
and to
our heavenly Mother,
the Holy Spirit,
in love and gratitude.*

Contents

Acknowledgements

I have been fortunate in being able to discuss my ideas with various friends and, in particular, I should like to thank Anthony Lovegrove, Edward Yarnold SJ, and Stephen Verney for their interest, criticism and encouragement. Thanks, too, to Charles Elliott, who found time to read and make helpful comments on the manuscript while filming on the Ivory Coast, and to Philip Law of SPCK for his encouragement and co-operation. Thanks to Bill Simpson for help with Semitic languages, and Ann Antrich for her help with Jewish theology.

While writing this book, much of my public worship has been at Guildford Cathedral, which is dedicated to the Holy Spirit. I should like to register my appreciation of the congregation of that cathedral for all they share with me, and thank the Dean, Alexander Wedderspoon, Sub-Dean, Peter Croft, and Precentor, Adrian Leak, for their friendship and support.

Thanks to my mother for her unstinting help with the practicalities of life; to Sophia and Zoë, the best daughters in the world, for all their love and laughter; and, above all, to Hugh, who shares so deeply and lovingly, not only in all I write, but also, in all that I am.

Acknowledgement is made to the following for permission to reproduce copyright material.

Faber & Faber and Harcourt Brace Jovanovich Inc. for the extracts from 'Ash Wednesday', 'Burnt Norton' and 'Little Gidding' by T. S. Eliot, in *Collected Poems 1909–62*.

Faber & Faber and Oxford University Press Inc., New York, for the extract from 'The Annunciation' by Edwin Muir, in *Collected Poems* (1965).

Grafton Books, a division of the Collins Publishing Group and Harper & Row for the extracts from e.e. cummings, *Selected Poems* (1960).

A. P. Watt Ltd., on behalf of Michael B. Yeats and Macmillan, for the extract from 'Maid Quiet' by W. B. Yeats, in *Collected Poems* (1963).

CHAPTER ONE

We Believe in the Holy Spirit

But through the endless afternoon
These neither speak nor movement make,
But stare into their deepening trance
As if their gaze would never break.[1]

IMMORTAL, INVISIBLE

One of the most popular subjects for medieval and early Renaissance artists was the annunciation story, in which Mary learns that she is to give birth to Jesus Christ. Anyone who has strained a neck muscle studying the frescoes in Florentine churches or pored over art books about this period will have been struck by the depth and intensity with which these early painters imbued their portrayals of this event.

One of the reasons for this quality lies in the fact that the annunciation did not 'happen' in quite the same literal sense as the nativity, crucifixion or Last Supper. These were events that were witnessed by a number of people, could be described in ordinary language and, eventually, recorded for posterity. The annunciation, however, while no less real, occurred in secret in Mary's heart. The story describes an ordinary girl 'conceiving' of the amazing fact that God could be human, and that to bring this revelation to birth Mary herself must bear the creator of the universe within her womb.

Angelic messages from God take a variety of forms in the Bible and it is often difficult to determine what was actually visually perceived. It may be that Mary's visitor was a human being bearing God's message, a friend putting in the right word at the right time; maybe there really was a flurry of wings and a shining light; or perhaps God's revelation grew within Mary's heart and came to fruition in the same way as the child Jesus was to do in the coming months. Whichever of these interpretations we find most convincing, what the artist was required to convey was a spiritual, rather than a physical, truth.

The essential sequel to the story is that it was through the operation of the Holy Spirit that Mary received God's Word; and artists, in attempting to portray the moment in which Mary was touched by the infinite God, had to struggle to depict the invisible, to represent the unseeable. What they found was that this mystical moment, stretching out beyond time, could best be represented in terms of Mary's relationship of love and trust with God. For while a casual onlooker at the event might fail to see the glory of an angel of God, Mary's human response is accessible to all.

We therefore see portrayed in the figure of Mary emotions that we recognize and with which we can immediately identify: love, fear, tenderness, wonder, horror, joy and obedience. We recognize these emotions because they are familiar to us in our ordinary lives, but we stumble against the limitations of our experience when we try to understand Mary's interaction with the angel. Only Mary herself could have said what form the bearer of God's message took.

We encounter a similar problem whenever we try to describe the Holy Spirit of God, for that which is spiritual rather than material cannot be seen. Indeed, we sometimes feel it is easier to span the gap of 2,000 years that separates us from the man Jesus, than it is to open our eyes to the Spirit of God at work around us now.

In theory, it might be possible to verify the facts of Jesus' life as recorded in the Gospels. But we lack much of the data for this, so that arguments will always remain as to whether the blind man really did regain his sight, how much bread was actually shared out at the feeding of the five thousand, and whether the rending of the Temple curtain was metaphorical or whether it required the attention of an ecclesiastical seamstress. But in all these cases what is at issue is something demonstrable, the truth or falsity of which makes some sense to us.

As we move from the recorded events in the life of the man called Jesus of Nazareth to the resurrection of Jesus Christ, our normal language becomes less reliable. We have seen in recent years that although belief in the resurrection is fundamental to our faith, deeply committed Christians can interpret this event in ways that appear diametrically opposed—depending on their understanding of such concepts as 'physical', 'spiritual', 'presence', and even the term 'resurrection' itself. However, even the resurrection is, in principle, open to investigation and it is just possible to conceive of new evidence coming to light that would force us to clarify our beliefs and arrive at a common understanding of the facts.

This is not, however, the case with the Holy Spirit. Although the Spirit of God appears throughout the Bible, the many references do not add up to a consistent theory that would describe this Spirit. In fact, Christian belief in the Holy Spirit as equal with God, part of the doctrine of the Trinity by which we try to comprehend the mystery of God, was formulated many years after any of the biblical writings were penned.

We find, in both Scripture and patristic writing, a great variety of ways of understanding the Spirit, as writers tried to make sense of their experience of God. No one invented the Holy Spirit. Over the years, different people tried to describe the experience of God in their lives and gradually evolved a vocabulary that went some way towards affirming what they knew to be real.

Those descriptions of the Spirit that survived, did so simply because they coincided with the experience of other people; they rang true. In other words, the doctrines to which we can give wholehearted assent were arrived at by the operation of the 'Aha principle'. This is the principle by which we come across something written or said, which we have not ourselves written or said before, which seems to express exactly what we think or feel, or represents what we would like to have communicated. Many people have this experience when reading poetry, of discovering lines that express their emotions so precisely that they almost feel they have written the lines themselves. Liturgy, at its best, inspires this response; while we pray the words that writers in the past, or liturgical scholars of the present, have created, the words become truly our own and express our deepest thoughts and feelings.

The very symbolism we use to explore our theological concepts differs according to the angle from which we are looking. For instance, the symbol of water for the Holy Spirit is far more vital in parts of Africa than it is in Europe or North America. To those who have lived with the threat of drought, the image of the Holy Spirit as life-giving water entering parched souls will convey more potently their experience of God the Spirit entering their lives than it will for those of us who groan when it rains on Saturday.[2] Although God does not change, our understanding of God is constantly changing to reflect our lifestyle, the state of society in which we live, and our understanding of what now is.

We are not trying to discover something new, but to find a way of describing what has always been, though it has never been, and probably never can be, completely understood. When Newton saw the apple fall he had a flash of comprehension that led to the theory of gravity. He was not inventing something new, or showing people events of which they had no experience, but positing a way of looking at the world that made more sense of it than had been possible before. The mathematical formulae with which he expressed this process were new, but gravity itself had existed since the dawn of time. Even Adam and Eve would not have expected apples to float upwards!

We are involved in a similar adventure as we try to make sense of our experience of the world we live in and the God who created it. Both the world and its Creator have existed from the beginning, but our understanding of them, in physical and spiritual terms, is part of a long process of discovery that is still continuing. In our enquiries into the nature of the Holy Spirit, it is therefore important that we look for an understanding of the concept which takes into account the insights of former ages but is also consistent with our present experience.

Although we have only limited biblical and doctrinal guidance, we must beware of swinging to the other extreme by imagining that the Holy Spirit is a brand-new entity which we are only now creating within the Church. The Holy Spirit was not born with the charismatic movement, or even with the Christian Church. In the first verse of the first chapter of Genesis we read that 'God's spirit hovered over the waters'; however and whenever our world came into being, the Holy Spirit was there at the beginning of creation.[3] We also believe that this same Spirit has been present in the lives of women and men ever since, inspiring and guiding them. But that which has always been, has not necessarily always been known or understood.

So on the one hand we are not looking for an ancient truth that was once understood and now has to be rediscovered; and on the other hand, our enquiry must be cradled within a history of thought that stretches back through time to the beginning of the world. Our task is to examine the concept in order that we might understand more, and thus come, through that same Holy Spirit, to a deeper relationship with God.

In this endeavour we shall obviously use the Bible to probe, to see how earlier people experienced the Spirit, to witness the power of the Spirit in history and in personal lives; but we will be disappointed if we expect the Bible to provide a set of ready-made answers. If we imagine that our understanding and vision must be constrained by written reflections on God's activity several thousand years ago, then the Bible serves us ill by interposing a barrier between us and the God whose children we are. If, on the other hand, our reading of the Bible helps us to discover the activity of God the Holy Spirit working in the world since the Scriptures were written, then it is inspired indeed and will lead us into ever greater knowledge and love of that God.

The witness of the Bible, in fact, is one of radical change and adaptation as people come to understand a little more of the mystery of God. The story is one of pilgrimage and discovery, of the wonder and excitement of continuing revelation. It is a description of humanity moving into relationship with God and it applies as much to humanity now as in the past.

As we come to perceive God 'moving with us', as our changing perception reveals more of the transcendent to us, so we shall come to fear change less when we witness it in the Church or in the world, and perhaps we shall begin to welcome it as inspired by God the Holy Spirit. To refuse to accept that God is continually being revealed through the process of history is to deny the Holy Spirit of God. How could we possibly revere everything contained in Scripture, including national-istic feuds and hatreds, and yet refuse to hear the prophets crying in our own twentieth-century wilderness, fail to see God's Spirit animating the young, the adventurous and the radical, and stop our ears to the Spirit's call that we enter into solidarity with the poor and oppressed?

Although we cannot see the Holy Spirit, we can become aware of the action of the Spirit. We cannot see the wind, that force which provides us with one of our most powerful metaphors for the Spirit of God,[4] but we can see the action of the wind both in the gentle swaying corn and in tempest-torn woods. We cannot see love, or even describe very accurately what it is, but we have no difficulty in pinpointing the effects of love, or recognizing the presence of love in a person. After the angel had left Mary, the power of the Holy Spirit came upon her and she conceived. In whatever way this conception took place, Mary did not see the Spirit, but the results of the activity of the Holy Spirit within her body soon became apparent for all to see.

A NEGLECTED DOCTRINE

The purpose of this book is to explore our concept of the Holy Spirit, and to suggest ways in which a fresh approach to the way we speak about the Holy Spirit might clarify our vision of God and make our faith more immediately relevant to our lives.

There is little doubt that our doctrine of the Holy Spirit is one of the least developed areas in mainstream Christianity. With a few notable exceptions,[5] there have been relatively few books or sermons on the Holy Spirit, and what are rather patronizingly called the 'excesses' of some charismatic Christians have only deepened the embarrassed silence that surrounds the subject in many churches today. But without a coherent understanding of the person of the Holy Spirit, we will have a limited view of God and fail to experience the riches available to us in the doctrine of the Holy Trinity.

Our failure to develop a satisfactory doctrine of the Holy Spirit, however, is not the only area where our understanding of God is deficient. Over the years we have also allowed a masculine bias in our theology to distort our vision of the deity. Efforts are now being made, in many parts of the Church, to overcome this defect, particularly within that branch of study known as feminist theology. Most feminist scholars work within a frame of reference that sees God as both male and female in perfect complementarity. They should not be confused with the small group of extremists who designate God as male and then reject him in favour of the Great Goddess. If the Church in general has failed to comprehend the full glory of God by limiting itself to a masculine image, those who now abandon the concept of a male God in favour of a Goddess figure fail just as fundamentally and for similar reasons.

Our vision of God will always be finite. There is little point in beating our breasts over the blind spots of our past. If we believe that revelation is ongoing, we shall not find it surprising that there are still new things for us to learn about God. There is now good reason to believe that Christians will gradually come to a more balanced, less masculine, vision of the infinite God. It is to be hoped that we shall at the same time open ourselves to a more vital belief in, and experience of, the Holy Spirit of God.

It is not enough that charismatic Christians, in their respect for the Holy Spirit, go some way towards compensating for the apathy of the mainstream churches. Nor can we fool ourselves that a proper appreciation of the feminine in God is the sole preserve of feminists. These are both aspects of theology to which all should be committed and which will be major areas of debate in the Churches in the coming years. It is hoped this book will contribute to that debate by exploring the extent to which femininity and the Holy Spirit are related. For as our concept of the feminine in God is refined by a study of the Holy Spirit, so also will our approach to that Spirit be deepened and expanded by our exploration of femininity.

Given the paucity of books on the theology of the Holy Spirit in general, and more particularly on our relationship with the Holy Spirit, it might be supposed that to embark on such a discussion is to enter the rarefied air of theological debate. Since most Christians are content to leave the finer points of doctrine to the theologians while they get on with the business of living, this would be to relegate study of the Holy Spirit to a position of a minority interest within the Church. This, however, would be to misunderstand completely the nature of the Holy Spirit, for our understanding of, and relationship with, the Holy Spirit is fundamental to who we are. It affects not only our thinking about God, but also our praying to God and our whole experience of living in God's world.

Thinking about God

To start with, unless the Holy Spirit is central to our theology we can have little idea of the nature of God or begin to enjoy a personal relationship with God. The God we worship is not some mythological deity around whom we weave fanciful stories, but is the God who created all that is, who loves us personally, who was incarnate in the person of Jesus Christ, and who lives within us now as the Holy Spirit. For the transcendent God was not only incarnate in the person of Jesus Christ, but is immanent now, and for ever, in the world.

The stories of creation and of the earthly life of Jesus concentrate on the action of God long ago in history. But the Holy Spirit is God here with us *now*. Unless we come to grips with God in the form of Spirit, we can make no sense of God present with us through all time, concerned and incarnate in the world. The Spirit of God still moves over the waters of our chaos, bringing in that new creation that is life in the Kingdom of God.

Praying to God

We do not come to know a loved one by studying a curriculum vitae, but by enjoying an intimate relationship. And in the same way, we come to know the Holy Spirit not in a theological analysis, but in that intimate meeting of God and humanity which we call prayer. Every time we attempt to pray, we face the paradox that the God we address is both far beyond anything that we can hope for or imagine and yet also closer 'is He than breathing, and nearer than hands and feet'.[6] It is an arrogance to suppose that there are any words we can offer that could be worthy of the eternal Creator. Yet Jesus told us, when we pray, to behave as though we were talking to a parent about all the things that concern us in life.

Trying to come to terms with this paradox is a problem for many Christians, and has led some to give up praying completely. Certainly, prayer as a struggle to communicate with a distant God, far beyond our comprehension, is a daunting exercise. Yet, if we can be aware of God the Holy Spirit in us and all around us, then prayer becomes an opening of ourselves to that Spirit, rather than a conversation with a distant deity. If we allow the Spirit to pray in us, communion with God becomes a natural, rather than an artificial, activity: 'The Spirit comes to help us in our weakness, for, when we do not know how to pray properly, then the Spirit personally makes our petitions for us in groans that cannot be put into words.'[7] It is only through the Holy Spirit that we can truly pray, and our most satisfying experiences of prayer are those in which we feel that prayer has transcended our efforts at stringing words together: that prayer has broken down our isolated individuality and allowed God the Holy Spirit to pray in us. In those moments we begin to know what it means to be 'in Christ', but it is the Spirit of Christ we encounter, not the human person of Jesus. Jesus Christ is risen, ascended and glorified. The Spirit of Christ whom we meet now is the Holy Spirit who lives in us. This is not a second-best alternative to meeting the man Jesus, for what we mean by the Holy Spirit is God as Spirit, meeting us, working in us, being God in our lives. We pray 'Thy kingdom come' because we long for life here and now to reflect the beauty and goodness of God.[8] The reason we believe this to be possible is that we are free to live in the Spirit of God and so to move, albeit falteringly, into the life for which we were created.

It is through prayer that we allow God to impinge upon our lives. We pray for the guidance of the Holy Spirit, for inspiration, comfort or a vision of holiness, and it is through the operations of the Spirit within us that we find that our prayers are answered. In intercessory prayer we pray for others, knowing that God the Holy Spirit is at work in their lives, healing, guiding, protecting. Through prayer we also come to recognize the Spirit of God in strangers and in enemies, in Christians who hold different views from our own, and in people of other religions. When we pray in this way, not only does prayer become more real, but it also dawns on us why it is so important to carry on praying: for prayer is intimately concerned with our living in the world.

Keep praying in the Spirit on every possible occasion.[9]

Living in God's world

This leads on to the third point, which is perhaps the most important of all, namely, that we believe the Holy Spirit to be the giver of life—all life.[10] The world is both created and sustained by God the Holy Spirit, in whom we live and move and have our being, whether we know it or not. When, at the end of the Eucharist, we pray 'Send us out in the power of your Spirit', we become aware of this life within us as we go about our everyday lives. So it is that, for the Christian, aware of the presence of God within, the Holy Spirit is not just a factor in a theological debate, nor simply the one through whom and in whom we pray, but the source of our being, vitally concerned with the details of ordinary life.

If God's Spirit is in us, then God is intimately involved in everything that matters to us: our families and places of work, our commitments and dreams, our fears and delights and failures. The Spirit of truth and holiness, of purity, peace and love, is in *us*, at work in our lives, and the distinction between sacred and secular completely collapses. The curtain of the Temple is torn from top to bottom.

We believe in the Holy Spirit, therefore, not because a group of good or learned men in history have recommended such belief, but because we experience the Spirit working in our own lives. Our concept of the Holy Spirit has more to do with our ordinary experience, our periods of struggle and darkness on the one hand or of simple happiness on the other, than with the formulation of doctrines and creeds; and the best test of whether we are guided by the Holy Spirit is to ask if we are being led to engage more fully in life, or to distance ourselves from it. For to live in the Spirit is to be at home in that world which is continually created and sustained by God's love.

The Holy Spirit is the activity of God in relationship with women and men, and as our experience changes so too will our understanding of the Holy Spirit. Even St Augustine, writing about the Trinity, realized that no one could have the last word on the subject: 'it is useful that many persons should write many books, differing in style but not in faith, concerning even the same questions, that the matter itself may reach the greatest number—some in one way, some in another'.[11]

This does not mean that God reflects us. God is infinite and all that we can ever say about the deity will fall far short of such a God. But we reflect God as we are able, and, as society changes, so we will become able to reflect different aspects of the infinite God that we had not grasped before.

In this book we shall explore some of the implications of taking seriously the doctrine of the Holy Spirit. For example, does the fact that the word used by the Hebrews to denote Spirit was a feminine noun shed any light on our understanding of the Spirit of God? Although a number of writers through the ages, from Macarius to Congar, have spoken of the femininity, and particularly of the motherhood, of the Holy Spirit, many of these writers have, in general, betrayed negative attitudes to women. It is therefore worth enquiring whether the feminine qualities that they claimed to recognize in the Holy Spirit have any genuine connection with the female, or are mere idealizations fed on fear of women. Does the ascription of femininity to the Holy Spirit simply mask an assumption that the Holy Spirit is inferior to God, an obedient handmaid to the male Father and Son? Or has it something to teach us about celebrating the fullness of masculinity and femininity in God?

Since the final formulation of the doctrine of the Trinity in the fourth century, it has been a basic tenet of Christian doctrine that the Holy Spirit is not an adjunct or subsidiary to God, but is *essentially* God. If we really believe this, then we shall strongly resist any attempts to split the unity of the Trinity. To recognize femininity in the Holy Spirit is to respond to the feminine in God.

The assertion that the Holy Spirit is God is not just a theoretical position, for our understanding of the Holy Spirit affects our relationship with God. To know God is to receive the Holy Spirit. To receive the Holy Spirit into ourselves is to incarnate God. But what does it mean to receive the Holy Spirit? The final chapters explore the imagery of breath or air as the origin of our word for spirit, and suggest that to receive the Holy Spirit, that gift available to all, is to live in God in the present moment. For since the doctrine of the Trinity states that the Holy Spirit is one with the God who was incarnate in human form, the Holy Spirit can be seen as the one who unites earth and heaven and enables us to recognize, and begin to live in, the kingdom of heaven on earth. We breathe the air of the kingdom of God.

Living in the Spirit, that spiritual dimension which is part of our human potential, involves living fully in this changing world that God has created, loved and redeemed. We shall therefore find that it is by entering fully into this life, in the power of the Spirit of God, that we become truly free.

CHAPTER TWO

Language, Church and God

Where has Maid Quiet gone to,
Nodding her russet head?
The winds that awakened the stars
Are blowing through my blood.
O how could I be so calm
When she rose up to depart?
Now words that called up the lightning
Are hurtling through my heart. [1]

LANGUAGE MATTERS

One of the major changes that has crept up on the Church in recent decades is the rejection of a chauvinism which, until a few years ago, was so well-established within Christianity that few were even aware of it. It was only when thinking people—particularly in this case thinking women—challenged established assumptions that the Church began to break through to a new and better way of talking about both God and humanity. In the same way that we are now astonished that our forebears were content to endorse slavery, so we are now moving slowly—and, at times, painfully—to a position where we will consider it incredible that the Church was one of the most stalwart bastions of male chauvinism for so many centuries.

This is not the right place to examine the reasons why many societies evolved in such a way that men achieved dominance and superiority over women, but simply to observe that even in some of the most entrenched of those societies the winds of change in the last century have been levelling out many of the worst excesses of such injustice. Whether one applauds or fears such fundamental shifts in our understanding of humanity, they are bound to affect our understanding of the God who created women and men in the divine image.

We live in a more equal world than that which oppressed our sisters and brothers in biblical, patristic and medieval times, and as our vision of humanity has broadened, so, necessarily, has our vision of the infinite God. As we live in a society that is gradually moving towards an equality of women with men, black people with white, physically handicapped with able-bodied, so we are able to take part in the exciting process of coming to see a little more of the wholeness and perfect goodness of the God who made us, and whose image, though frequently tarnished, is imprinted on all women and men.

As women have come to realize their inherent dignity in society and in the Church, they have become more aware that the attitudes that have robbed them of their rightful place for so long are encapsulated in, and propagated by, a masculine bias in the very language we use to communicate. Language is the vehicle of thought and the concepts we form are conditioned and limited by the language we employ. For example, Eskimos have an extended vocabulary of words that denote the different qualities of snow. Because they have the linguistic tool with which to make such differentiations, Eskimos perceive clear distinctions where English speakers recognize no difference at all. Small children do not learn to talk in order to express a fully developed system of rational thought: rather, they learn the activity of rational thought through acquiring, in language, the counters for playing that particular game.

The philosopher Wittgenstein has drawn attention to the way in which language influences thought;[2] in a rather different vein, the anthropologist B. L. Whorf[3] has demonstrated how the language of the Hopi Indians in America affected their understanding of modern physics. But such insights are not restricted to scholars. Even quite unsophisticated television audiences will pick up the connotations hidden in a reference to 'the wife' or 'the mother-in-law', and will expect the man who uses such language to exhibit a certain form of behaviour towards women.

Much of the anger experienced by Christian women in recent years stems from their frustration at finding themselves involved in playing a game, the ground rules of which keep changing at the whim of the opposing party. This can be seen in both the areas of language use that are increasingly found to be causing offence to women.

Daughters of God?

The first of these relates to the use of terms that describe the human race in general, and the Church in particular. When girls first began to question the chauvinism of the Bible translations they were comforted by being told that, simply for the sake of brevity, the term 'man' is used to stand for 'man and woman' and that 'mankind', which really means 'human beings', has no masculine connotations at all. But the assurances that nothing hung on this choice of nomenclature gradually began to appear specious as these women grew to womanhood in the Church and found that in reality a great deal hangs on it, namely, the whole edifice of authoritarian church structures. It became clear that, although more than half its members are women, the Church assigns a vastly different value to women and men—so much so that many parts of the Church cannot conceive of ordaining women to their ministries.

As society changed, and women were able to assume more equality in other walks of life, it dawned on them that their religious life was in danger of being thwarted by the refusal of the Church to acknowledge their equality with men. Half a century or so ago the Church had the exciting opportunity of leading the world in its attitude to human rights and value by outlawing sexist attitudes and language. One of the tragedies of Christian history is that instead of blazing the trail, the Church will finally suffer the indignity of being dragged by the hair—kicking and screaming, behind all the more willing institutions of society—to a position more consonant with belief in a loving and just God.

As women became more aware of their own worth, they also became dissatisfied with terminology that categorized them as surrogate men. We have now reached a stage in most churches where exclusive male language causes deep offence, not just to a militant feminist minority, but to the majority of women present. There is no doubt that such language used to be considered to refer equally to men and women. However, language usage changes, and today the same language that formerly appeared innocuous is now seen as betraying and sustaining deeply sexist attitudes. Contrary to what some men believe, most women delight in their femininity and have no desire to be subsumed under the category of men. For women to be addressed as 'Dear Brothers' or 'Sons of God' is extremely insulting, and assurances that God made 'man' in his own image or that Christ was incarnate 'for us men and our salvation' do nothing to persuade women of God's love for them.

It is most unfortunate that liturgical scholars were not more awake to this development of language when services were being revised in the 1960s and 1970s, for the new liturgies contain a number of examples of exclusive language which will necessarily call for more changes within the next decade.

Despite the attitude of the Church as a whole, there have been clergy who have displayed great sensitivity and consideration for women in the words they have used in prayer and liturgy. Although their independence of spirit was not always appreciated, these clergy are now being vindicated as the rest of the Church examines the assumptions implicit in the use of exclusive language.

The Roman Catholic Church, for instance, is reviewing all language used in worship. The Vatican Congregation for Divine Worship issued a directive in 1987 that the use of the word 'men' in the prayer of consecration over the chalice should be dropped with immediate effect, and that other examples of such limiting language should be scrutinized. As was pointed out in this document,[4] to abandon the masculine emphasis is to render a more faithful translation of the original Latin, which includes reference to neither 'vir' nor 'homo'. In other words, there is no basis for the implied sexism, and has never been any excuse for its use. As the Roman Catholic Church is now demonstrating, once the awareness of the injustice has dawned, there is no great problem in correcting the errors.

The light of revelation appears to be dawning, too, on the Anglican Church which, in the latter months of 1988, accepted that there are severe problems associated with the exclusively masculine language so often employed in church circles.[5] Although the recognition of sin does not lead to its expurgation overnight, and the debate will have to grind its way through a number of (male-dominated) synods and committees, there is now good reason to hope that offensive language will be purged from the liturgies within the next few years.

In the meantime, individuals can help to outlaw the discrimination by taking unilateral action, which need be neither difficult nor costly. Many clergy and lay people are now discovering that nothing is lost in sense or rhythm by changing the offending words or omitting them altogether. For example, even when singing the Creed, 'for us all and for our salvation' fits the music just as well as 'for us men and for our salvation'; in the invitation to intercessory prayer it is perfectly acceptable to use the phrase 'let us pray . . . for all people according to their needs'; and to pray that we might 'honour one another', instead of 'honour all men', might be a first step towards respecting women.

Most black people living in Britain or the United States know the power of language to affect attitudes and behaviour. The eradication of racism begins with an onslaught on derogatory epithets used to denote racial type for, in any society in which racial description can be used as an insult, a mental attitude is produced in which racial abuse is a possible outcome. It is this principle that caused Mahatma Gandhi to reject the term 'Untouchables' for members of the lowest caste in India and to refer to them, instead, as the Harijans, or 'children of God'. The use of the name 'Untouchable' was outlawed in India in 1949 and in Pakistan in 1953 and, although the caste system still operates widely in the sub-continent, the lot of the Harijans has improved considerably.

Parents generally recognize this quality of language intuitively when they teach young children to say 'thank you' and 'sorry', not just because these words are culturally respectable, but because the act of speaking such words increases the chances of inspiring the attitudes expressed by them. If we stop to thank someone for opening a door for us, or for preparing a meal, or sending us a postcard, we sow within ourselves seeds of genuine gratitude. A child who has been persuaded to apologize accepts some responsibility and culpability for his or her actions, and also implies an effort to avoid that behaviour in future.

A teacher who consistently addressed one member of a class using infantile language would soon instil in that pupil a low self-esteem; a questionnaire form that asked for a description of marital status under the headings of 'single, married or widowed' would increase the sense of rejection experienced by divorcees; and clergymen who, from ignorance, indolence or bigotry, do not bother to resist the sexism implicit in exclusively masculine language give a clear and unambiguous message to the world about their attitude to women.

This has not always been the case, for sensitivity to language gender is a modern phenomenon; and it is arguable that we should not impose modern rules on the language of the past. But it must now be recognized that the use of language has changed and that an irreversible process has gathered momentum. In the same way as black people who have experienced racial prejudice are quite reasonably sensitive about the association of the colour black with negative qualities, women today are no longer content to be addressed as surrogate men. There is no point in regretting the change in language sensitivity; it is simply a fact of life. Although some people might consider it highly inconvenient to adapt linguistic terminology in order to remain in tune with the changing consciousness, they will soon discover that insularity is sadly out of place in language, where the prime intention is communication with others.

Our heavenly Mother?

The other area of language usage where women feel cheated is in the adoption of masculine terminology to refer to God. This problem is greatly exacerbated, in the English-speaking world, by our inability to discuss the personal nature of God without ascribing gender.[6]

Assurances have been offered that in God there is neither male nor female. It has been conceded that it is regrettable that there is no word that embraces both genders but, since one does not exist, women must not be offended by the use of the pronoun 'he' to refer to God. Added weight accrues to this position since Jesus himself referred to God as 'Father', or, more accurately, 'Daddy', while as far as we can tell from the records available to us, he never used the feminine equivalents of these terms in addressing God.

But once again, the assurances have proved vacuous, for the designation of God as male has in fact concentrated our minds on masculine qualities in the deity to the exclusion of feminine ones, and therefore diminished our vision of God. Much has also been made, in the ordination debate, of the contingent fact that God in Jesus was a man and that somehow, by implication, God is therefore slightly more male than female.[7]

It is difficult to use the pronoun 'he' of someone and then resist the temptation to perceive that being as having masculine qualities. 'God's a good man', said Dogberry in Much Ado About Nothing. If we use exclusively masculine terminology to refer to God, we perceive Godhood itself in a particular way. It is around that perception that we form the value systems that influence our own behaviour in the world, responding to the cultural norms and assumptions that form the context for our thought. For example, the kind of response to life elicited by belief in a stern judge or a God of wrath is completely different from that inspired by belief in a loving, accepting mother.

We shall see that the Bible uses feminine, as well as masculine, images for God, who is, on occasions, described in terms of tenderness and compassion. Also, some of the greatest Christian thinkers, such as St Anselm and the Lady Julian, have valued the experience of turning to God as a mother. Like Mary Baker Eddy, a hundred years ago, many Christians now feel comfortable addressing the deity as 'Father–Mother God'. However, this does raise some problems both in terms of its cumbersomeness, and in the fact that it conjures up two different sets of associations within the same expression. For this reason, it may be psychologically more fruitful to refer sometimes to the motherhood, and at other times to the fatherhood of God.

In recent years awareness has grown of the limitations to our concept of God that are implied in sexist language, and also of the injustices that cloaks acceptance of such language in respectability. As this awareness has increased, women within the Church have begun to express their pain and anger. A number of women have left the Church, but others have stayed on, believing that if they can remain strong in love they will bear fruit; fruit that will not only enable them to reach fuller spiritual maturity and self-respect, but will enlarge everyone's perception of God and lead to the enrichment of the whole Church. It is within the context of these women's struggles, as well as the more general dissatisfaction of Christians with a cock-eyed perception of God as male, that we should examine the hypothesis that we can meaningfully refer to God the Holy Spirit in the feminine gender.

OUR CHANGING EXPERIENCE OF GOD

We shall explore, in Chapter 3, the way in which the early Church had to grapple with the nature of the relationship between Jesus Christ and God the Father. As the concept of the Trinity evolved, Christians were able to incorporate the Holy Spirit, through whom they experienced God, into the doctrine, and trinitarian theology gradually became the rock on which the edifice of the Church was built. Unfortunately, because God was perceived as Father and Jesus Christ as Son, the habit became entrenched of referring to God in all aspects as male.

The disadvantages of using masculine terminology to refer to God soon began to make themselves felt, resulting in the development of some of the more extreme forms of Mariology in an effort to compensate for the imbalance. But in the same way as a 'token woman' on a committee can exacerbate the male dominance that it seeks to alleviate, so this introduction of a compensatory feminine aspect into religion drove our conception of God deeper into masculinity.

Our theology today must continue to underline the indivisibility of the infinite God in terms that allow us to conceive of God as both omnipotent and personal, and that relate to our experience of life and understanding of the transcendent. But humanity has changed over the centuries, and the formulation that the early Fathers found to be all-embracing might well be inadequate to reflect the experience of people nearing the end of the twentieth century. If doctrine is couched in language that does not grow out of our reality, it will not be very surprising to find that it impinges minimally on the lives of ordinary people.

As individuals and as a society, we are now more aware than ever before of the need for balance between masculine and feminine, and men as well as women are realizing that they are deprived of the fullness of God if they are constrained to conceive of God simply as male. The whole world rejoices in the balance of male and female. If Father, Son and Holy Spirit are all allowed to collapse into maleness, the Trinity can no longer embrace that integration of female and male which we perceive to be the norm throughout nature and which finds expression in our own personalities. If God were entirely and unrelievedly masculine, then it would be nonsense to expect women to relate to 'Him' in the core of their beings. Conversely, men who responded to God in passionate love, such as St John of the Cross, would have no choice but to express themselves in homosexual terms.

Resolving the problem is not so straightforward in the case of the language we use of God as it is when we describe humans in sexist terms. People quite clearly come in two different flavours, male and female, and no society that purports to respect all members equally can subsume one under the other. We are fortunate in that our language allows us to use collective nouns which include women and men on an equal footing—'people' can refer to a group of women, men, or a mixture of both. But we have no pronoun with which we can refer to God without assigning a gender, unless we adopt the neuter 'it', which would rob God of personhood and equate the Almighty with inanimate objects. This would destroy the vital truth that the doctrine of the Trinity seeks to preserve, which is that we can enter into meaningful relationship with God. But if we settle for the exclusive masculine terminology that we have inherited from earlier ages, we at one stroke disqualify half the world's population from any awareness of having been created in the image of God.

Experiencing the Spirit as feminine

This is one reason (though not the only one) for exploring the possibilities and implications of addressing the Holy Spirit in the feminine gender. Because fewer scholars have written about the Holy Spirit and because few of us have learned to pray to the Holy Spirit, we have not been so indoctrinated into speaking about that Spirit in masculine terms. However much we might wish to address God as our mother, we must accept that many Christians find it difficult to accustom themselves to the notion of the God of the Old Testament as 'she'; and unless we are of the spiritual maturity of Julian of Norwich, we find it slightly jars on our linguistic sensibilities to follow her in using 'she' when referring to Jesus.

Exploration of this option, however, does not diminish the excellent work now being done to introduce feminine language into theology more generally. Writers like Janet Morley[8] are enriching our experience of God through their appreciation of the feminine at work in the whole creative process. God is not neutral, but whole, and new metaphors that concentrate our attention on the vulnerability and tenderness of God, on the pain of bringing to birth in creation, on identification with the dispossessed and the powerless, will enlarge our vision of the infinite God.

But while both 'Father' and 'Son' are intrinsically masculine words, I believe there is a strong case to be made for conceiving of the Holy Spirit as feminine. This has been recognized by a number of writers before, but in general they have drawn back from the consequence of this revelation: that it is appropriate to address the Holy Spirit in the feminine gender. Their reticence has generally stemmed from a fear that such language in some way divides our concept of God.

Some feminist writers also object to the ascription of femininity to the Holy Spirit on the basis that this is just a sop to women. Their arguments appear to stem from a belief that the Holy Spirit is derivative from God and in some important sense inferior to God the Father and Son. We shall see, in Chapter 4, that this is a deeply mistaken assumption and that, on the contrary, to accord femininity to the Holy Spirit embeds the female at the very heart of the Godhead.[9] Indeed, it is no more divisive to conceive of the Holy Spirit as feminine than it is to contain both Father and Son within the Trinity.

If we truly believe in the unity of the Trinity, an appreciation of part of that Trinity in feminine terms will give a more complete picture of the God who transcends our divisions of gender; it will help us to redress the balance in our understanding of God, away from the chauvinist assumptions that have been our diet for so long; and it will enable us to address God in the feminine gender without artificiality. It will also enable us to concentrate on some of the qualities of God that have traditionally been perceived as more feminine, so that, for instance, we can grow in trust as we rest in the loving arms of God and take sustenance from our mother. While it will be necessary to take a critical look at what we mean by 'feminine' and 'masculine',[10] we shall find that many of the qualities that are ascribed to the Holy Spirit accord with characteristics which, in our culture and time, are more appropriately designated feminine than masculine. It should however be emphasized that I am not claiming that the Holy Spirit *is* female, but only that it is helpful for us to comprehend her in that way.

To adopt feminine language to refer to the Holy Spirit will help us to break through those limitations of language that have belittled the deity, and cheated us of at least half of what we are able, at this point in history, to understand of the nature of God. It would clearly be inconsistent to deny that God is male and then to assert that the Holy Spirit is female. To keep this in mind, then, it might be a good idea on occasion to use 'he' to address God while speaking of his motherhood; and use 'she' for the Holy Spirit and then accept some of the masculine attributes of the Spirit as well as the feminine. For the intention is not to split God. God is eternally one and indivisible, and the parts of the Trinity describe the same God—even if they are clothed in sexually differentiated terminology.

This problem of God-talk is one that will concern us all in the coming years, and it is my hope that the adoption of feminine terminology when referring to God the Holy Spirit will go some way towards freeing our language from those constraints that at present limit our vision. My study of the Bible, of early Christian writings and of poetry and art, as well as my personal experience, have all led me to believe that to address the Holy Spirit in the feminine gender is both natural and illuminating.

To refer to the Holy Spirit as 'she' is now as natural to me as the designation of God the Father as 'he' was throughout my early years. I hope that those who do not yet share this vision of the Holy Spirit will not find this use of language shocks too much for them to join in the adventure of exploring our concept of the Holy Spirit. For it will become apparent that understanding the Spirit in feminine terms is a means to an end, not an end in itself. To those offended by the idea that one can address the Holy Spirit as 'she', I extend sympathy, and hope that the experience will bring them some understanding of, and empathy with, those women who can no longer belong to the Church because they are so offended by the perpetual assumption—which does not tally with their experience—that God is male.

It is not my purpose simply to change the way people address the deity. The most appropriate way of addressing the mystery of God is, after all, in silence, and it is far more important for Christians to explore that option than to proliferate words and cerebral arguments. But I hope that by exploring some feminine aspects of the Holy Spirit we may come to a fuller understanding of the place of that Spirit within the Godhead and celebrate the Holy Spirit as truly God. As we do that, we may come to understand the intimacy of the relationship that the Spirit enables us to have with God, and find that we are freed by the Spirit to live more holy lives in the world as we live more fully in God.

CHAPTER THREE

The Eternal Triangle

one's not half two. its two are halves of one;
which halves reintegrating, shall occur
no death and any quantity; but than
all numerable mosts the actual more

minds ignorant of stern miraculous
this every truth—beware of heartless them
(given the scalpel, they dissect a kiss;
or, sold the reason, they undream a dream)[1]

TRINITY IN THE NEW TESTAMENT

Before considering what it means to conceive of God the Holy Spirit in feminine terms, we should look at the way in which Christians came to understand the Holy Spirit as one with the indivisible God: co-equal and co-eternal.

The doctrine of the Trinity provides us with a clear example of the continuing revelation of God, since it was arrived at by a gradual process of trial and error many years after the books that were included in the canon of Scripture were written. On no occasion does the New Testament use the word 'Trinity', and it does not seem to have occurred either to the Gospel writers or to the authors of the Epistles to encourage Christians to think in terms of trinitarian belief.

There are two or three oblique references in the Epistles to a growing awareness of the divinity not just of Jesus Christ but also of the Holy Spirit. For example, the first Letter of Peter opens with a reference to all three persons of the Trinity,[2] and in the first Letter to the Corinthians, Paul, on at least two occasions, appears to have in mind something approaching an equality of Father, Son and Holy Spirit.[3]

Apart from these vague allusions, there are only two direct references to Father, Son and Holy Spirit in the New Testament in terminology that we would recognize as trinitarian: one said to emanate from the mouth of Jesus and the other from the pen of St Paul. The first comes at the end of St Matthew's Gospel, where we find Christ sending his disciples out into the world: 'Go, therefore, make disciples of all the nations; baptize them in the name of the Father and of the Son and of the Holy Spirit, and teach them to observe all the commands I gave you.'[4] Given the single occurrence of this particular formula in the Gospels, it is unlikely that these were the actual words spoken by Jesus. As far as we know, at no time during his ministry had Jesus linked these concepts together in this way or taught his disciples to understand the nature of God in such terms. By the time Matthew's account of the life of Christ came to be written, the Church had embarked on the process of creating liturgies, and this particular trinitarian expression was most probably a well-known formula from one of the early baptismal liturgies.

The Pauline instance occurs at the end of the second Letter to the Corinthians,[5] where a similar formula appears: 'The grace of the Lord Jesus Christ, the love of God and the fellowship of the Holy Spirit be with you all.' Once again, it is more than likely that Paul is here quoting a well-known liturgical formula, which, in fact, we still use today. However, even if these examples represent the very words spoken by Jesus or written by St Paul, these two references would not be sufficient to form the basis for the whole complex set of ideas that we call the doctrine of the Trinity.

The Trinity, then, was not part of the original gospel message, nor was it a bright idea that descended with the dove at Pentecost. It was a response to the serious problems people found they faced when they attempted to articulate their concept of divinity, particularly the divinity of Jesus Christ.

Although few people appear to have realized it during Jesus' life on earth, the experience of those who were with him at the end of his life and who remained faithful to him in the following weeks led them to believe that Jesus was more than a good man—more, even, than the promised king who would free the Jewish race from Roman domination. They came to believe that he was the incarnation of God. This became the central tenet of Christian belief, marking it off from Judaism, and it has characterized Christianity ever since.

It was natural that it should be the christological problem that was uppermost in the minds of the first Christians, for the idea that God could be human was a completely new part of the religious equation which had to be fitted into faith structures inherited from the Old Testament. By concentrating on different texts, it was possible to perceive Jesus as anything from a man who received a special mission through his baptism, to the God who was before all things and who created the world. Even St Paul himself, who was in no doubt at all that Jesus was the Christ, appears to have varied in his opinion as to whether the Christ was equal with the Father or subordinate to him.

In the Old Testament writings it was never anticipated that the promised Messiah would be God in any sense. 'Messiah' simply meant 'the anointed one' and, quite apart from the fact that he was expected to be a saviour in political or military terms, all hope was directed towards a special man with a mission, not to an incarnation of God.

The marvel of the Christian message was that sending a special envoy was not enough to show the extent of divine love. Only through total self-giving in the life and death of Jesus Christ could God express infinite love and demonstrate the worth of human beings in the eyes of their Creator. This was the good news that had turned the world upside down for the first Christians, and that appeared to be running like quicksilver through the Mediterranean world, but it was not a message that could be comfortably embraced without fundamentally adapting existing patterns of belief.

Paul therefore had to grapple not only with the necessity to assert that the Messiah had come, when most of the religious leaders he respected denied this, but also with changing quite radically the concept of what the Messiah was. It was for this reason that we can, on occasions, detect a slight prevarication creeping into his writings, suggesting, particularly in the first Letter to the Corinthians, a non-equality of Son with Father.[6]

There was a mystical attraction in the number three in the ancient world, but it would also be true to say that the early Christians did experience God in three quite distinct, and equally powerful, ways. They read in their Scriptures about the God who created the world, and they lived within a tradition that had worshipped this God since time immemorial. That they had no desire to change. However, they had also seen and touched Jesus, and had gradually come to understand that this man who had lived and died among them was, in some strange way, God. It had dawned on them that this was the same God whom they already worshipped but with whom, through the life and death of this man, they had now entered into a completely new kind of relationship.

As though coming to terms with this change of spiritual gravity were not enough, they also discovered the power of God entering their lives in a manner they had not previously envisaged as they became vividly aware of the action of the Holy Spirit. This reversal of traditional ways of understanding the deity must have been momentous for a group of people who made no pretensions to theological or philosophical enquiry, but who found themselves forced by events to expand their concept of God.

Recognizing the divinity of Jesus Christ and the Holy Spirit did nothing to alleviate the problems for these Jews, since the unity and indivisibility of God was absolutely fundamental to their religion. The Shema, the sacred text carved closest to the Jewish heart by daily repetition, stated: 'Hear, O Israel: The Lord our God is one Lord.'[7] They could not therefore conceive of the three manifestations as three distinct Gods. How could they remain true to their deepest theological convictions, and at the same time respond to the truth as they were now able to perceive it? This tension was to characterize Christian thought throughout the early centuries, until the Cappadocian Fathers in the fourth century brought about an uneasy resolution in the final formulation of the doctrine of the Trinity.

BALANCING THE TRIANGLE

Neither of the most commonly used Christian creeds insists that we should 'believe in' the Trinity as such, and they are both rather over-economical in their description of the Holy Spirit. The earliest, the second-century Apostles' Creed, claims belief in the Holy Ghost in its final paragraph, along with belief in the Church, the Communion of Saints, the Forgiveness of sins and the Life everlasting.

This rather bald statement does nothing to define what the Holy Spirit is, or what it means to believe in the Spirit, and it was later expanded by the bishops who met at the Councils of Nicea in A.D. 325 and Constantinople in A.D. 381. This fourth-century Creed thus states more clearly the Christian belief in the Holy Spirit as part of the divinity, along with the Father and the Son, and goes on to describe some of the properties ascribed to the Spirit: 'Holy, Sovereign and Live-giving; who proceedeth from the Father; who with the Father and the Son together is worshipped and glorified; who spake by the prophets.'

Between these two creeds lies a whole history of hypothesis and dispute, ranging from the creditable to the disreputable. Embedded within this history we find the names of some of the great scholars and saints of the early Church who, far from playing intellectual games, were prepared to suffer insult and ruin in their search for truth. We also find a number of heresies, and might well be forgiven for suspecting a degree of arbitrariness in what became accepted dogma and what was condemned as heresy. Certainly, those who propounded the 'heresies' were every bit as committed to the gospel as their orthodox brothers, as intelligent in their theological study, and as keen to relate their theories to the Scriptures.

The document that most clearly encapsulates the final formulation of the doctrine of the Trinity is the Athanasian Creed, which was not composed until the fourth or fifth century:

> And the Catholic Faith is this: that we worship one God in
>   Trinity, and Trinity in Unity;
> Neither confounding the Persons: nor dividing the Substance.
> For there is one Person of the Father, another of the Son: and
>   another of the Holy Ghost.
> But the Godhead of the Father, of the Son, and of the Holy
>   Ghost, is all one.

As well as admiring the ingenuity with which the problem was eventually resolved, it is also important to appreciate the passionate nature of the whole debate. This was not an arena for academic games, but the very stuff of fundamental beliefs which affect the way people lived. Sarah Coakley, in her contribution to the Church of England Doctrine Committee's report, *We Believe in God*,[8] argues that 'it is the experience of prayer, both personal and corporate, which is our primary access to God as Trinity'. If this is so, then it is hardly surprising that the issues should have been so hotly debated by early Christians whose lives, she claims, were completely steeped in prayer.

Doctrinal differences

The formulation of the doctrine of the Trinity in the Creed was also, later, responsible for the first major split in the Christian Church, that between East and West, which is generally known as the Great Schism. In 1054 the Pope, Leo IX, and the Patriarch of Constantinople, Michael Cerularius, excommunicated each other and thus clinched what had appeared inevitable for some time: the complete separation of the Eastern and Western Churches. Having diverged, the two Churches developed in their independent ways, growing further apart as time went on. This split has never been healed, though few would now get excited about the major controversy—the 'filioque' clause—that tore the Churches apart.

In the Nicene Creed the Fathers had asserted that the Holy Spirit proceeds from the Father, basing this on the words of Jesus in St John's Gospel:

> When the Advocate comes,
> whom I shall send to you from the Father,
> the Spirit of truth who issues from the Father,
> he will be my witness.[9]

In the face of the Arianism still prevalent in the Church,[10] the word 'filioque' 'and from the Son' was added to the Nicene Creed in Spain in the sixth century to confute this tendency by reasserting the divinity of Christ. The Eastern Church accepted neither the political assumption that the West had authority to change accepted church dogma unilaterally, nor the theological innovation that appeared to compromise the supremacy of God the Father as the source of all.

The disagreement hinged, not on the divinity of the Holy Spirit, but on discussion of the relative merits of using the terms 'begotten' or 'proceeding from' to describe the relationship of the Holy Spirit with God. As Gregory of Nazianzus pointed out, to pursue the logic of generation to its limits lands one in the unfortunate position of having to accept that the Holy Spirit is either the brother of Christ or the grandson of God. But 'procession' did little to clarify the issue and most theologians have balked at distinguishing between 'generation' and 'procession' in any meaningful way.

TRINITY OR TRI-THEISM?

The danger with the doctrine of the Trinity is that it tends to fragment rather than unify our concept of God. Its purpose is really to help us comprehend the unity of God but, by giving us bite-sized pieces, it allows us to separate these pieces out and imagine that they can be served at completely different meals. At its best, the doctrine of the Trinity offers us the concept of the triune God and thus allows us to understand and adore the unity of God. But the Church has frequently failed to appreciate the full glory of this unity and, by concentrating on the separate parts as though they were different deities, has fallen unconsciously into 'tritheism' instead—with the result that other religions, such as Judaism and Islam, have never been persuaded that Christianity is monotheistic, since it appears to them to recognize and celebrate three gods.

This tendency is well illustrated in a number of trinitarian hymns, in which we address the different persons of the Trinity one after another as though they were separate entities—rather like Daddy-bear, Mummy-bear and Baby-bear in the story of Goldilocks. As well as drawing sharp lines between them, we always treat them in exactly the same order, first Father, then Son, then Holy Spirit, as though we might disturb some divine hierarchy if we changed them round. But if each is God then it should not matter in the slightest which we refer to first. The fault is not corrected, but rather compounded, by adding a final verse that addresses the Trinity itself; for it is God we worship, not a mathematical formula.

The doctrine of the Trinity relates to our understanding, not to the being of God, in the same way that correct spectacles improve our sight but do not alter the world around us. Our minds are finite so we need to take account of the limitations of our logic and mathematics in our theology, but God is not limited by such human concepts. There is not 'a Trinity' in the same way as there is a European Community or a USSR. There *is* God and we try to comprehend a little of what God is by means of our concept of the Trinity. In terms of mathematics, the Trinity does not work: quite clearly one and three cannot be identical. So why is it that we try to idolize our mathematical formulae by imagining that the Trinity is in some sense God? Far from blocking our spiritual progress, the formula is meant to be a stepping stone to take us further on into the mystery of God, which is far beyond numerical concepts.

What the Bible demonstrates is that God is constantly changing form in order to get through to us, appearing to some as an angel, to others as a cloud, to others as a burning bush. God is revealed as the deepest wisdom of the world, as a suffering dying man, as wind, or words of commonsense addressed by someone we know and love. God is all these things and many more because the infinite God is necessarily in all. All that changes is the way in which we perceive and receive God.

All three terms of the Trinity are traditionally used to stand for activities of God: the Father being the one who creates, the Son the one who redeems, and the Spirit the one who sustains. There are, however, other activities of God that are not covered by these terms, and it would appear reasonable to use different terms to apply to these activities and adopt the same concept of 'persons' to cover them. So one might choose to speak of God the mother who nourishes us, God the sister who lovingly teases us, God the friend who will not let us down, God the lover who pours himself into us.

But as long as the doctrine of the Trinity can be used to serve our understanding and faith rather than to rule them, it is every bit as valuable to us now as it was to the early Church Fathers. What I should like to offer are four ways in which we can use the Trinity to enhance our Christian faith and life but which avoid the pitfall of idolatry of the doctrine. In each case, I see more value in an approach that meditates on the mystery rather than engages in philosophical struggle with the concept.

Trinity as relationship

The first of these interpretations is certainly not new, but was explored by St Augustine in the fourth century in his book *De Trinitate*. In this work, written at a time when the doctrine of the Trinity was still not fully developed, Augustine tried to describe the relationship between the different ways in which we understand God. Using the human analogy of mind, its knowledge of itself and its love of itself—or perhaps more clearly comprehensible the lover, the object of love and love itself—Augustine conceived of the Holy Spirit as the spirit of love that joins the Father and the Son and draws women and men into communion with God.

The value of this approach is that it forces us to think in terms of relationships and therefore of community. Before creation, when all that existed was God, God existed in a loving community of harmonized co-equality. If this is so, then humanity, created in the image of God, is created for harmonious co-equal community. If the Church concentrated more on this and less on erecting an authoritarian institution claiming monopolies of truth and salvation, it might find itself able to enter into a deeper understanding of the nature of God through meditation on the Trinity.

This is something that is entirely consistent with the new vision of God which Jesus Christ brought, for he taught that God is love, that the very being and nature of God is love; and love is essentially relational. Easier though it would be, love is not something that can exist in isolation or abstraction, but it must come to grips with close encounters with real people. So only in our own loving can we live in the image of the God who is love. That is one of the reasons why our failures in love cut us off from God, for neither hatred nor stony individualism allows us to reflect the image of the God who is defined in terms of loving relationships.

A number of Orthodox icons are based on this relational interpretation of the Trinity, including the famous fifteenth-century Russian icon of the Old Testament Trinity by Andrei Rublev.[11] In this, the three characters sitting at a meal together are the three men who visited Abraham at Mamre in Palestine.[12] The writer of Genesis refers to these visitors collectively as God, though numerical consistency does not appear to have been a major objective in relating the story. Sometimes the three together are called Yahweh, while at other times they are conceived of as three individuals—Yahweh in the company of two angels. The import of the story, however, is that God appeared to Abraham in human form and that there were three persons. This could therefore be understood as a very early reference to the trinitarian nature of God.

Orthodox icons do not always represent the Trinity in this form: sometimes they portray the baptism of Christ, indicating the Trinity by means of the hand, the man and the dove.[13] At other times the setting is Pentecost, and the Trinity is represented in physical form by portraying Jesus Christ at the right hand of God and the Holy Spirit descending to earth. This again emphasizes the relational properties of the Trinity.[14] Another popular way of indicating the Trinity in Orthodox iconography is through the Transfiguration of Jesus on Mount Tabor, where Jesus is seen in the company of Moses and Elijah.[15] In most of these cases, what the painter has created is a meditation on the loving and harmonious relationship that exists within the heart of God. Some twentieth-century artists have adopted a similar approach in relation to the family group. So we find, among Picasso's paintings and Henry Moore's sculptures, meditations upon the oneness and yet distinctness of a family group, or a mother and child.

If taken too far, this understanding of the Trinity obviously runs into the danger of tritheism, for we envisage a family made up of separate individuals. The family is one, but the members are multiple. When we encounter this danger, it means we have gone far enough down that path and must change to another image.

Trinity as integrated personality

The labels we carry depend to a large extent on our relationships with others, with the ways in which different people see us. Thus one woman can be a lover, a mother and a lecturer, while being one and the same person. Each of the labels is an accurate, though partial, description of her, and each will be understood by at least one group of people. Similarly, the names we give God will depend on the way in which we relate to God.

It is interesting to reflect that one of the common Hebrew names for God in the Old Testament is *Elohim*, which is the plural form of *El*, or *Eloah*. Singular words are, in a way, far too limited to be used to refer to the majesty of the infinite God. Similarly, in the creation story in Genesis we find the writer putting into the mouth of God the words: 'Let us make man in our own image'. It might be objected that this is just an interesting example of the use of the 'royal we', rather than a claim to plurality. But perhaps the use of the 'royal we' is itself a recognition of the different aspects within the regal personality—for instance, the private and the public.

What the doctrine of the Trinity proposes is that however many aspects of God one may relate to, they are blended within an integrated personality and should not mislead us into worship of a pantheon of deities. Through meditating on the mystery of the three in one, it may be that we can also learn to keep the different aspects of our own personalities integrated, rather than pigeon-holing the various parts of our lives. Although we perform different actions and use different words depending on whose company we are in, we can only be truly at peace if there is an inner integrity that allows us to know ourselves to be the same person and to be recognizable as such to other people.

Trinity as koan

Instead of fighting against the difficulties inherent in the doctrine of the Trinity, it is possible to use them to advantage. One of the ways in which Zen Buddhists sometimes seek enlightenment is through meditation on an unanswerable question or paradox, called a koan. The activity of our minds can sometimes get in the way of contemplative player; one of the objects of the koan is to bring the mind up against a brick wall, thus stopping it in its tracks.

One of the most common of the koans is the question: 'What is the sound of one hand clapping?' Another rather more theological one is: 'If all comes from the One, what does the One come from?' I have long felt that one of the most fruitful uses of the doctrine of the Trinity is as a koan, where our minds, instead of arrogantly partitioning God in our game of intellectual riddles, is brought face to face with the unknown mystery of God and sinks into awed stillness. To do this, it is necessary to lay aside the convoluted explanations as to what the Trinity might mean, and instead to meet the concept head on: 'God is one; God is three; God is not divided; one and three represent the same God'. By taking the koan seriously we may come to the appropriate response: silent wonder and contemplation of the mystery of God.

Trinity as credal symbol

The fourth way in which one may approach the doctrine of the Trinity is as a summing up of our faith. The creeds that we recite in church are fairly long and complicated and cannot easily be held whole in the mind as we go about our ordinary lives. But if our belief is to influence our lives, we want to hold the essentials together in a way that will help us to pray at any moment of the day and will constitute a check against which we can test our other thoughts. The doctrine of the Trinity provides just such a symbol, for it sums up the major elements of the Creed in a compact and relevant form and makes them come alive for us.

The doctrine states belief in the God who creates, whom we therefore refer to as Father, the one from whom all comes; it recognizes God as one who loves and suffers in the form of Son; and it celebrates the Holy Spirit as the one who inspires and indwells. These activities of God can be recognized in our own experience, so that through the doctrine of the Trinity we can live out the meaning of our Christian belief. There are other things that God does in the world and in our lives, but these three certainly give us a pretty clear idea of the nature of the God we worship. By wrapping them up so concisely in the form of this doctrine, we are able to carry the whole Creed as a sort of mantra and pray the essence of the Creed by meditating on the Trinity.

Having acknowledged the late development of the doctrine of the Trinity, examined some of the advantages and pitfalls of espousing such a doctrine, and explored a few possibilities for using the doctrine today as a positive tool in practising the Christian life, we will now look in more detail at the concept of the Holy Spirit as part of the divinity of God within the Trinity.

CHAPTER FOUR

God Is Spirit

you only will create
(who are so perfectly alive) my shame:
lady through whose profound and fragile lips
the sweet small clumsy feet of april came
into the ragged meadow of my soul. [1]

PERSONHOOD

The Holy Spirit is described as the third 'person' of the Trinity and, unlike some of the other terms that pepper our theological language, 'person' is still a common noun in regular use. But the word 'person' is far from ideal in the context of understanding the complex nature of God.

The development of both philosophical enquiry and the modern discipline of psychology have changed the meaning of the word 'person' in directions that the early Church Fathers could not have imagined. One consequence of this is that modern thinkers approaching this subject are constrained by an understanding of the term that is ancient and undeveloped, and find themselves compromised by having to put aside much of their education and understanding of personal identity.

The Latin word 'persona', which was used to translate the Greek 'hypostasis', literally means that through which something is sounded. It originally denoted the mask worn by actors in the theatre and, by extension, came to refer to the actor's role. The word therefore suggested the being of the actor as understood by a certain audience, and in this limited archaic usage provides a useful way of describing our differing experiences of God. This analogy was favoured by some of the Church Fathers as a way of explaining how Jesus Christ 'was' God, so that Clement of Alexandria, for instance, was able to claim that Christ 'assumed the human mask'.

If we say that Laurence Olivier was Hamlet, Romeo and Archie Rice, we mean that he was those people in the context of certain plays at certain times. Within a particular context he was thoroughly that person, so that when he played Hamlet it would have been unthinkable for him to break the constraints of Shakespeare's play by, for example, marrying Ophelia and living happily ever after. So we believe that God was Jesus in first-century Palestine, and was therefore constrained by the context of that time and place, of human ignorance and the limitations of maleness. But this is a 'person' of God, a way in which we are enabled to see a little of that divine transcendence that by definition cannot be seen or even grasped in entirety by human beings. So we also believe that God was not diminished by incarnation, any more than Laurence Olivier lost his family connections, his education or his car by 'being' the Prince of Denmark.

But to say that God is Spirit is to say more than that on some occasions we are aware of God as Spirit. Rather, we believe that to be Spirit is the very nature of God; indeed, that any departure from the norm of spiritual communion with God, as when people have 'seen' God with their physical eyes, is the exception rather than the rule. The reason why we must worship God in spirit is that that is the reality of our relationship with God, who is necessarily spirit. But this is not to make our relationship with God distant or abstract. On the contrary, it is because God is spirit that we are able to enter into a personal and intimate relationship with what would otherwise be an unapproachable deity.

SPIRIT AS PERSONHOOD

John Taylor, in *The Go-Between God*,[2] suggested that not only are 'father' and 'son' metaphors when applied to God, but that 'spirit' is as well. In so far as we interpret spirit as breath, then the 'Holy Spirit' is a metaphor that allows us to understand something of divinity by reference to our own human experience of breathing. In the same way, all 'inspiration', not just of the Holy Spirit, is metaphorical, as also is 'enthusiasm', which literally means filling with God. But the distinction between spirit and matter is one that has real meaning and significance for us, and when we say that God *is* spirit, this is true in a more literal sense than when we say God *is* a father.

The Hebrew word *ruah*, breath, which we translate as spirit, was used by the writers of the Old Testament to denote the animating principle in both God and human beings. When used of people it does not convey some strange ethereal quality that is separate from their physical nature. It denotes neither an optional extra for the religiously minded, nor a sturdy homunculus which will be released from imprisonment when the body dies.

It means, rather, that which gives life and personality and meaning to a person. It is what makes a creature a recognizable human being, with all that that implies. In the second of the creation stories, for instance, God fashions a man from the dust and then breathes life into him. With that inspiration of breath, man is differentiated from inanimate creation and becomes a human being capable of love and communion with God. One of the implications of this myth is that to be alive, to have breath, is to have the propensity to be spiritual. The same could be said of Ezekiel's vision of the valley of dry bones.[3] When, on Ezekiel's command, the dry bones became human bodies and those bodies received the breath of life, it was in order that they could then enter into relationship with God. 'I shall make breath enter you, and you will live. I shall put sinews on you, I shall make flesh grow on you, I shall cover you with skin and give you breath, and you will live; and you will learn that I am Yahweh.'[4]

Because we are human we are animate; we have spirit and can relate to God. Conversely, death was associated with the departure of the spirit, and a common euphemism for dying was 'and his spirit left him', or, as occurs in the Gospels in describing the crucifixion, 'and bowing his head he gave up his spirit'.[5] Indeed, Christians still adopt this usage on occasions, particularly in greetings within some versions of the liturgy, when one person says to another: 'The Lord be with you', to receive the response: 'and with thy spirit'. This reply is not addressed to one distinct part of the person, and is nonsensical unless interpreted in the form in which it is expressed in more recent rites—to mean 'and with you'. In other words, a person's spirit is understood partly in terms of personal identity: it is that which makes someone the person that she or he is.

This, according to Paul, is also the case with God: 'After all, the depths of a man can only be known by his own spirit, not by any other man, and in the same way the depths of God can only be known by the Spirit of God.'[6] Rather than trying to define Spirit in terms of personhood, it might therefore be more fruitful to recognize that at least within certain contexts—such as among the ancient Hebrews whose thought forms still pervade our Scriptures—personhood can be more accurately defined in terms of spirit. We are aware of the 'personality' of God simply because we are able to relate to the Holy Spirit.

The ancient Chinese concept of 'chi' might shed some light on our own concept of spirit, for this life force in Chinese thought is also more than the physical presence of breath. When one takes part in the contemplative dance, the Tai Chi Chuan, one is learning to control and use one's breath, but along with that goes control and use of one's whole emotional and spiritual potential.

William Blake, the English poet, painter and visionary, rejected dualism,[7] not by denying the spiritual side of individuals but by subsuming the physical to the spiritual. For him, 'Man has no Body distinct from his soul; for that called Body is a portion of Soul discern'd by the five senses', so that what a person is depends entirely upon the spiritual. But Blake was considered eccentric by his contemporaries and his views have gained little currency since; in an increasingly materialist age the whole vocabulary of spirit became suspect.

SPIRIT OF GOD

In time, the dualism that crept into our understanding of humanity began to infect our view of divinity as well. This arose as a direct consequence of the doctrine of the Trinity, which had been formulated for the express purpose of maintaining a unified understanding of God.

Such a division of God would have been anathema to the ancient Jews, who used 'God' and 'Spirit' synonymously. When the writer of Genesis tries to describe how it was 'in the beginning' we read: 'And the Spirit of God moved upon the face of the waters.'[8] We are certainly not meant to construe this as a division of labour in the divinity. It means simply that before all else was, God moved.[9] The Old Testament takes for granted the fact that God is Spirit and only later moves from that first principle to the revelation that God is Father and Son.

This synonymy is so widespread throughout the Old Testament that it cannot represent simply a romantic tendency among the writers of theology or poetry, but rather the way in which these people conceived of the God whom they believed to be not an idol made of wood or metal, nor an individual human person, but divine Spirit. It is not just in the Pentateuch, but also in the Psalms, the Wisdom writings and the Apocrypha, that we find the term 'Spirit' frequently being used as another way of addressing or referring to God: 'Cast me not away from thy presence: and take not thy holy spirit from me.'[10] 'The Spirit of God has made me, and the breath of the Almighty is giving me life.'[11] 'I am with you—it is Yahweh who speaks—and my spirit remains among you. Do not be afraid.'[12] 'Thou didst speak and all things came to be; thou didst send out thy Spirit and it formed them.'[13] Later, in St John's Gospel, Jesus was to spell this out even more unambiguously when he defined God in terms of Spirit.[14]

To speak of God in this way is the only way in which we can make sense of the concept of God. It is through the Spirit that we know God; the reason for this is not that the Spirit is an adjunct or emissary of God, but that since God is Spirit then Spirit is the very Being of God. It is difficult to know what could be meant by God being something other than Spirit, and when we pray that we may go out 'in the power of your spirit', what we mean is 'filled with you'. For God the Holy Spirit is both giver and gift, in the same way as God incarnate in Jesus Christ is also both giver and gift as he lays down his life for his friends.

What is amazing about the Pentecost experience, in its historical form and in the lives of Christians today, is that we do not just receive a 'gift', we receive God. Our spirit, our personhood and all that we are, is filled with God, so that, as a necessary by-product, we receive power and joy and overwhelming love and all those other phenomena that shook the disciples out of their old lives. But it is God who comes to us, in our wholeness as people who 'have spirit' and can therefore enter into relationship with God. So when, in the Aramaic mantra prayer, we repeat the word 'Maranatha' ('Come Lord'), this plea is addressed to the whole of God, not part. Similarly, at the epiclesis, when we 'call down' the Holy Spirit on the elements, it is God whom we invoke.

It is possible for us to come, on the strength of the evidence displayed around us, to a belief in a loving Creator. We read the Gospels and are inspired by the record of those who could remember the man Jesus. But our present experience of God, our relationship with the transcendent, is of God the Holy Spirit. This is the aspect of God that we see in action in the present; for in the same way that we have observed spirit in human beings to be the animating life force, so, in the case of God, the Holy Spirit is divine energy. We become aware of this energy in the wonders of constant creation, our breathtaking glimpses of infinity and our tender contemplation of the tiny flower. We also meet God the Holy Spirit in relationship with others, for the spirit moves between people, constantly incarnating God.

SPIRIT OF CHRIST

The birth of Jesus Christ was foretold by means of the name 'Immanuel', which does not mean 'from God' or even 'Son of God', but 'God with us'. So in the life of Jesus of Nazareth, God the Holy Spirit became incarnate, took on human life. When, however, St John describes this mystery in poetic language he does not suggest that the Spirit was made incarnate, but that the Word was. John did not, of course, have an understanding of God based on trinitarian theology and was not attempting to split the deity into separate components. For him, if the Word was 'in the beginning', was 'with God' and 'was God', then the Word *was* Spirit.

Word and breath are intimately related. Without breath there can be no word, for every word we utter is a pattern of vibration on the underlying breath. By its very nature breath cannot be static but, like wind, must move; so only through the giving out of breath can the word be delivered. If we take this analogy from physics into our picture of God, we see the breath of God, the Holy Spirit, moving in the world and issuing as Jesus Christ the Word of God.

The 'Word', which gives form to thought, is that which is the true expression of what is in the heart. Through words we can make public what is deepest and most private to ourselves; only when others have heard or read our words can they understand what is going on within us, who we are. Through our words we offer reasons, explanations and descriptions of ourselves. One way of interpreting John's use of this concept, therefore, is that Jesus Christ, the Word of God, is the key to our understanding of God.

God does not need the Word, for in God is the silence of perfection, the depth of all knowledge and truth. But humanity needed the Word, in order to come to some understanding of the nature of God. The explanation that was offered was absolute rather than partial, for the Word was with God and the Word *was* God. So it was that the discourses related by John, in which Jesus describes himself in a series of different images, are built on the rock of the 'I AM', the name which, according to the Old Testament writers, God used to describe himself.

It is because of what has been revealed to us in Jesus Christ that we are able to understand God in terms of love and self-sacrifice, and that is precisely why Jesus is the Word of God: he is what makes sense of God for humanity. Part of the revelation, in fact, is that in the same way as we understand Jesus to be a child of God, so also are we children of God, through the same Spirit of God who was in him. It is not that our status changes with the incarnation, that God suddenly decides to adopt us, but that, through the Word, *we* come to understand more of what God is and what we are. 'The proof that you are sons is that God has sent the Spirit of his Son into our hearts: the Spirit that cries, "Abba, Father", and it is this that makes you a son.'[15]

Once the Word, Immanuel, had made it clear to us that God is with us, that we ourselves are involved in the great I AM, then the spirit could continue to live within us, to be God with us. So the coming of the Holy Spirit at Pentecost was the natural consequence of the incarnation of Jesus. Further, the God who was incarnate in Jesus is one and the same God with the Spirit who entered the disciples' consciousness at Pentecost: 'at the moment when he said that the Spirit would be sent, Jesus promised that he would come himself'.[16]

Paul is able to equate the presence of Christ in a person with the presence of the Spirit, and there are several passages in the Epistles that imply that the Holy Spirit and the Christ are one and the same: 'if Christ is in you then your spirit is life itself'.[17] So Paul is able to refer to the Spirit of Jesus, or the Spirit of Christ, in unambiguously pneumatic language: 'the help which will be given to me by the Spirit of Jesus';[18] 'and I live now not with my own life but with the life of Christ who lives in me'.[19]

There is also some evidence to suggest that Jesus himself spoke in such terms to his disciples, as when he urged them to relax and trust the Spirit when they were in difficulties. This admonishment occurs twice in Luke's Gospel: the first time the disciples are told that the Holy Spirit will teach them what to say; and the second time it appears that Jesus himself will inform their speech: 'When they take you before synagogues and magistrates and authorities, do not worry about how to defend yourselves or what to say, because when the time comes, the *Holy Spirit* will teach you what you must say.'[20] 'Keep this carefully in mind: you are not to prepare your defence, because *I myself* shall give you an eloquence and a wisdom that none of your opponents will be able to resist or contradict' (my italics)[21]

God comes to us as and where we are able to perceive. God came to a group of first-century Jews as Jesus of Nazareth, but, having provided the key that could bring human beings closer to God, Jesus said, 'Do not cling to me'.[22] For the purpose of the key, the explanation, or the Word, was to enable us to see God, not Jesus himself. The Gospels make it clear that Jesus regarded himself as a means to an end, and eschewed any form of Jesus-worship. He came to bring people to God. And, if a motley group of women and men from Palestine followed him and learned to see God through him, that was solely that they might pass through the partial to the whole.

Having demonstrated through his life, death and resurrection what God is, Jesus then ascended. However literally or metaphorically we understand Luke's story of the Ascension, the implication is that Jesus departed from the disciples, still trying to raise their eyes to God. This Word of God then came as the Holy Spirit, because God is Spirit and by receiving God, human beings were able to enter fully into the experience of God.

PENTECOST AS THE FULFILMENT OF INCARNATION

The coming of the Holy Spirit is the whole point of the incarnation. Without it, the story of Jesus might have qualified for inclusion among the great and beautiful stories of the world but would not have impinged on our lives. Through God the Holy Spirit living in Jesus, we learn that God is with us; and as we receive that same Spirit we discover the reality of God's being with us, in us, living, working, suffering and loving through us. We are in God because we share the Spirit of God.

Perhaps it was only when God's people had received the Word and come to a more mature understanding of the nature of God, that they could be Spirit-filled. A few individuals had been granted fleeting experiences of this before, and these characters illuminate the pages of the Old Testament; but with Christ it became possible for all to receive the Spirit. Jesus Christ was filled with the Spirit because he was one with God. Through this union of human and divine he gave power to all people to become children of God. His whole life, therefore, not just his death, was an act of atonement, since it brought about the possibility of people being at one with God. This is a reality still experienced by Christians today when they are filled with the Spirit and made one with God.

One of the problems that has sometimes bedevilled our theology of the Holy Spirit is the apparent difference between the way the Spirit is portrayed in the Old and New Testaments. But once 'God' and 'Spirit' are reunited this problem evaporates, for those writers who had witnessed Jesus Christ had come to a new and fuller knowledge of God and therefore, necessarily, to a new and fuller knowledge of the Holy Spirit, who was incarnate in Jesus. God the Holy Spirit remained the same, but our understanding of God the Holy Spirit had changed radically through what we had seen of Jesus Christ, God incarnate.

This realization that God really *is* one, and that attempts to subdivide divinity into three diminish our conception of God, does not mean that we should abandon the doctrine of the Trinity. If it is seen as bringing together our disparate ideas about God, then it is as valuable as it has ever been. The Gloria, for example, instead of being a worn-out formula tagged on to any other prayer, can become, particularly in the form in which it is sung by the Taizé community, a thrilling love song. In the same way as we load epithets on to a human lover, trying to express the fullness of our love, so in approaching God we can enjoy piling on the different titles, building up a picture of the ways in which we feel confident to relate to God.

Gloria, gloria, gloria,
patri et filio;
gloria, gloria, gloria,
spiritui sancto.[23]

The singing of such a joyful love song is a natural and wholehearted response to the infinite God whose being and nature is love. But this is not a love that is subject to those artificial boundaries of gender which constrict the lives of human beings; since God made male and female in the divine image, both must be contained within the wholeness and harmony of the infinite God.

CHAPTER FIVE

What Is Femininity?

Patience is a virtue,
Possess it if you can;
It's seldom found in women
And never in a man.

Discussion of the gender of God frequently founders on the rock of confusion between whether someone or something is female or feminine, male or masculine. It is therefore worthwhile attempting to clarify these terms, in order to avoid misunderstanding later on. If we assert that because traditionally the Holy Spirit is one who shelters and nourishes us, who is tender and compassionate, who dances and plays and who indwells and brings peace, does it follow that the Holy Spirit is displaying feminine qualities? If the Spirit *does* display feminine qualities, does that mean that 'she' is female?

FEMALE/FEMININE AND MALE/MASCULINE

The word 'female' refers to biological function and is the determinant of sexual type; 'feminine' is a description of certain attributes, which can be either personal qualities or modes of behaviour. 'Feminine' can also be used to describe a person who possesses these attributes to a certain degree. To be an adult female logically implies that one is a woman, and it is, barring the most unusual circumstances of a sex-change, part of one's unalterable nature. To be feminine, however, is to be reputed to have certain qualities or modes of behaviour which can, within limits, be modified. Thus, a female may not necessarily be feminine, and someone who displays feminine qualities may not be a woman.

It would, therefore, in theory, be quite reasonable to claim that the Holy Spirit has feminine qualities, but is in fact a male. This would be close to some Victorian artists' portrayal of Jesus—as a feminine male with flowing hair and soft features, more at home in the company of lambs and pretty children than driving hucksters out of the temple. Conversely, we are led to believe that the legendary Amazons were masculine females, a concept that struck terror into the hearts of some of the boldest of Greek warriors. But, of course, all we mean when we describe the Amazons in such terms is that, within the conventions of what our society considers masculine and feminine, they would appear masculine. In other words, masculinity and femininity are culturally determined.

In the vast majority of cases, there is no room for dispute over whether someone is female or male. It is an observable, testable fact. There are hermaphrodites, but they too are defined by reference to the norms of male and female. There, is, however, no such consensus of opinion over whether someone is feminine or masculine. Even when there is agreement within one society, there are still fundamental differences between cultures.

BIOLOGICALLY RELATED MASCULINITY AND FEMININITY

Difficulty arises, therefore, over knowing how far the biological differences of female and male are responsible for the qualitative differences of femininity and masculinity. It would be surprising if millions of years of evolution, in which clearly differentiated biological types were essential to the survival of the species, should have failed to instil in women and men personal qualities that are most appropriate and adaptive to their different biological purposes. Yet, strangely, it is difficult to delineate qualities of femininity and masculinity to which all women and men conform, in the universal way that all conform to femaleness or maleness.

For instance, men, on average, are physically stronger and have louder voices than women, and some 'masculine' qualities reflect these differences between the sexes by implying that men are socially dominant or more forceful in arguments. In the past, strength undoubtedly gave men certain advantages. However, in our technological age, brute force is not so frequently required of human beings, who can now lift immensely heavy loads by flicking a switch, or wreak vast destruction by simply pressing a button. Thus this biological difference is gradually becoming less relevant to the qualities of gender.

Some feminists believe that the childbearing characteristic of females has changed as much as reliance on superior strength by men, since with the development of reliable contraception no woman need conceive a child if she wishes not to. But the analogy will not hold, for it is not a necessary part of the definition of maleness to be strong: if men are on average stronger than women then many men will in fact be weaker than many women, while being no less male. But even if a woman never bears a child, or even if for some medical reason it is impossible for her to bear a child, her femaleness is still defined by reference to the childbearing potential of her physical make-up. To be female rather than male means that within the reproductive cycle necessary to preserve the future of the human species, one falls on one side of a particular line rather than the other.

Another way of appropriating femininity and masculinity to sexual differentiation has been by attempting to associate *masculine* and *feminine* with the roles of the different sexes in sexual intercourse. So the more active and giving qualities have been designated masculine, and the passive and receptive ones feminine. But this tendency is based on a very partial view of sexual activity which, even if it reflects the sexual mores of an earlier age (which is by no means certain), is not consonant with the experience of sexually active couples today. Women can be as active in sexual intercourse as men, and it is arguable that what they produce and give is as necessary as the seminal fluid that they receive. Women also, of course, exemplify giving in their biological functions of childbearing and feeding, in which they give of themselves to another. Further, increasing acceptance of homosexual liaisons has allowed us to understand something of the interchangeability of sexual roles and warned us against stereotyping the roles and behaviour of the sexes in intercourse.

In order to tie *feminine* and *masculine* to sexual role, one might return to the fundamental images of dolly-goddess and phallus which have been important symbols for human beings since prehistoric times. To understand femininity in terms of rhythm, fecundity, nurturing and softness, and masculinity in terms of hardness, impregnation and dissemination, would allow some room for qualities that are biologically based. But even biological differences can be misinterpreted. Many small-breasted women who have been conditioned by the expectations of society to connect milk production with breast size have been pleasantly astonished at the onset of lactation to discover themselves better equipped for breast-feeding than many of their more heavily-endowed sisters.

Nevertheless, there are one or two qualities that could be claimed to be related to biological type. For instance, aggression is associated with the presence in a person of such androgens as testosterone. Since this hormone is present to a greater degree in men than in women, then aggression would seem to be an innate masculine quality, with masculinity here identified with maleness. Some would argue, too, that the maternal instinct that appears quite early in the young female is not simply culturally determined, but is a consequence of the female body 'being programmed' to give birth, perhaps by the presence of oestrogens.

In so far as aggression and the maternal instinct relate to such physical accidents of maleness and femaleness, they could be said to be innate to women and men independently of the fact that some men are not aggressive and some women do not exhibit the maternal instinct. By extension, one might then feel able to claim that aggressive tendencies will contribute to the development of courage, and that the presence of the maternal instinct will lead to gentleness, so that these two qualities would then be designated masculine and feminine respectively. But again, this quality distribution is far from universal.

SOCIALLY RELATED FEMININITY AND MASCULINITY

However, many characteristics that are designated feminine or masculine are at a further remove from biological differences than are the aggressive and maternal instincts, and are in fact the consequence of living in a particular society. 'Feminine' frequently means nothing more or less than that which accords most closely with the cultural norm for the female, and 'masculine', that which accords most closely with the cultural norm for the male. But the fact that certain characteristics are culture-determined does not mean that they can be ignored for we are shaped by society nearly as much as by our genetic inheritance. It may be necessary to work to change unattractive features of the *status quo*, but it will not be very surprising if language reflects the current assumptions of our society. If we lived in a counry in which men ate women, then it might well be a common misapprehension that an important feminine quality was that of being 'good to eat'. It would be more fruitful in this situation to prevent men eating women so that they no longer had the concept of what they might taste like, than to attempt to alter the language while leaving the behaviour intact.

Cultural or social femininity in some cases arose as a consequence of the biological. For instance, in primitive societies it was more convenient for women to nurture infants, as they were likely to be caught up in a fairly continuous cycle of childbearing. It then followed that women, tied to home by the responsibility of raising children, should develop skills and propensities for home-making in which their creativity and management skills could be exercised despite their confinement. Men, on the other hand, were free to leave the home and thus it fell to them to provide for their families in much the same way as many male birds and animals have to provide for theirs. So such occupations as hunting and farming became dominated by males who were in no danger of succumbing to the restrictions of pregnancy and childbirth. These cultural differences, we have already noted, have been altered by such factors as contraception and technology. The nest of qualities and behaviour patterns that they described may still be adhered to by many individuals, but they can no longer be sexually determined in a simplistic way.

Since we are to a great extent formed by the societies in which we live and of which we are a part, there might well be characteristics of femininity and masculinity that have been bred into women and men in much the same way as aggression and maternity have been by evolution. For instance, given the centuries in which men were the breadwinners and women the home-makers and child-rearers, it could have become part of the male personality to be more single-minded and for the female to be more holistic. As more women work outside the home and more men tend families, this conditioning will be modified so that in time it might no longer be true to make such a differentiation on the grounds of gender. But that would not affect the observation that, at this time and in this culture, such characteristics have a gender-determined quality. So while these non-biological uses of masculinity and femininity must be recognized as being entirely dependent upon the historical and cultural context, and in some cases we have every reason to seek to change them, that does not render them impotent or artificial as descriptive terms.

Some personality differences between women and men arise simply because of opportunity. For instance, it might be argued that within our society women are less conformist than men, but this is probably only because men have in the past more often been subjugated by working regimes than women, who have, while 'bound' to the home, also benefited from a degree of freedom and autonomy. Conversely, some claim that men possess greater leadership skills than women; again, this is likely to be simply a consequence of the fact that they have had more opportunity to exercise such skills.

Negative uses of feminine and masculine

An examination of the ways in which the terms 'masculine' and 'feminine' occur in conversation will reveal that they are frequently used as value judgements. To observe that someone is female or male is morally neutral: to ascribe femininity or masculinity is value-loaded. Thus, if a woman is feminine, that is deemed to be a good thing, but a man with the same characteristics might be criticized for being effeminate. A man with masculine characteristics is respected, while a woman with those same qualities can be derided with the epithet 'butch'. A variation of this principle has arisen in recent years by the introduction into the language of the word 'macho' to describe men in whom the masculine qualities are considered excessive; in general, this term is used by women to indicate that exaggerated masculinity is not attractive. However, there does not appear to be a corresponding word for men to describe women in whom there is an overabundance of femininity.

'Feminine' literally means 'to do with women' and 'masculine' 'to do with men', but there is little agreement over how much of human personality and behaviour falls within these categories. As we have questioned our assumptions about women and men in the last few decades, so we have come to the rather surprising conclusion that we do not actually know what is inherently connected with being a woman or a man. Many of the uses that were hallowed by long tradition were found to betray a desire by each sex to exclude the other from full partnership in life. Women, as well as men, have been guilty of this chauvinism, by using such phrases as 'masculine insensitivity', or asserting that to have a one-track mind is a masculine trait. Language of this sort has as little to contribute to harmony and progress as such equivalent male chauvinist phrases as 'feminine gossip' or 'feminine interests like housework and fashion'. Used in these ways, *masculine* and *feminine* become negative terms which lead to gender-stereotyping, and are used predominantly to limit the activities of the opposite sex.

The terms have therefore been misused to exclude members of one gender group from areas which, according to the expectations of that particular culture, are the preserve of the opposite sex. This can be done either by repressing people's natural inclinations by making it unacceptable for one or other sex to feel certain emotions, or by disqualifying them from professions that they are otherwise well-qualified and motivated to pursue. It is only by refusing to be bound by this limiting use of the terms that we have come to realize that men can be nurses, and that women can drive lorries and hold key political posts. There is, however, still more work to be done in freeing the gender-specific words from the accretions of ignorance and prejudice with which they have become encrusted over the years, so that they may be colourful and descriptive without being constricting.

Clearly, any ascription of femininity to the Holy Spirit that was based on value judgements, or that sought to exclude men from full life in the Spirit, would diminish rather than expand our view of God. Exclusivity can have no part in our response to the Holy Spirit, who, as we shall see later, is the one who liberates rather than restricts.

It transpires, then, that the terms 'feminine' and 'masculine' are used in vastly different senses. They can refer to characteristics that occur in the different sexes because of biological factors that are unlikely to alter. They can describe particular behaviour patterns that have been observed over many generations, but which might well change in the future. They can be used metaphorically to cover those aspects of personality that have a logical or poetic association in our minds with biological function—as, for instance, when a powerful speaker impregnates an audience with new ideas, or, as in Plato's imagery, a philosopher acts as midwife to help people bring their own ideas to birth. 'Feminine' and 'masculine' can also be used to assert the expectations of a particular society. For example, in Western civilization the appreciation of textile art is sometimes considered to be feminine because women have traditionally created clothes; but, as more men find they enjoy knitting, embroidery or dressmaking, so the feminine connotations will be winkled out of these activities. Finally, 'feminine' and 'masculine' are used to expressprejudice and thus constitute a form of attack on the opposite sex—as, for instance, when it is claimed that women are woolly-headed and illogical, or that men cannot understand emotion or express their feelings.

FEMININE AND MASCULINE QUALITIES

It is true that different sets of qualities do appear to be aligned and might reasonably be subsumed under a common category. For example, there is some connection between the qualities of gentleness, passivity, poetic sensibility and faithfulness, or between courage, analytical reasoning, strength of mind and objectivity—in that an individual will tend to have several qualities from the same list. But in reality that person is no more likely to be of one sex than the other. If certain qualities and activities are allowed to 'belong to' females in an exclusive sense, then the proliferation of such feminine qualities and activities will systematically circumscribe what is possible or desirable for the female. If it is unfeminine to analyse, to define or to insist on one's rights, then women will never be sure what it is to be a woman or persuade men to accept them on their own terms. Conversely, if weeping is designated a feminine activity, then men will not be able to weep—however much nature or psychology demands that they should.

We have, in fact, inherited from the East a pair of identifying terms that adequately cover those qualities commonly divided into masculine and feminine, as well as many others. 'Yin' and 'yang' can be used to differentiate between many pairs of opposites. Each one builds up a collection of related terms; they are value-free, and together they make up an harmonious whole. These might therefore offer a more useful pair of opposites than the traditional masculine/feminine ones, which are so loaded with prejudices. Femininists rightly object to essentialist language that limits women's self-realization by assuming that qualities that are traditionally referred to as feminine have some necessary connection with women. If the traditional opposing pairs of qualities were divided into yin and yang, we could eliminate the words 'masculine' and 'feminine' from our vocabularies.

But the terms we use did, in fact, originate in observation and expectation relating to gender. The qualities that are said to be feminine originated in the female, either in what were once observed to be biological characteristics, or what at a particular time and in a particular place was the social role of women. That does not mean that these qualities occur only in women, but simply that it is in that group that we have isolated and identified the qualities.

If we refer to someone having a very English sense of humour, we do not mean that only the English have this attribute; we mean that it has been observed and identified clearly among the English, and can therefore be extended as an illustrative concept to other groups of people. One might find many Europeans who exhibit an Eastern stillness and wisdom, but the way in which we first identified these qualities was by reference to the many Asians in whom they were clearly observable. Many French people are dowdy and many Americans elegant, but when we describe someone as having 'French elegance' we are denoting as French the quality of elegance, not the person who possesses it. We are saying that this particular quality of elegance can be identified by reference to a group in which we believe the quality can be most easily identified and observed. Thus, whether or not a particular quality is essentially or contingently associated with one gender, it is through a concentration of the quality in that one sex that we have, in the first place, learned to perceive it at all.

Positive qualities associated with gender

Qualities traditionally designated feminine might include: vulnerability, tenderness, patience, faithfulness, compassion, sensitivity, intuitiveness and poetic sensibility. The masculine list might include courage, analytical reasoning, logic, assertiveness, single-mindedness and ambition. Yet most people would agree that all of these qualities are possessed and exhibited by both men and women.

There is, therefore, considerable disagreement as to whether the qualities we call 'feminine' or 'masculine' have anything to do with the femaleness or maleness of the person with those qualities. 'Essentialists' believe that there are basic differences between the sexes which are reflected in the kinds of qualities they exhibit. 'Accidentalists', on the other hand, deny any inherent connection between sexual type and qualities of personality, claiming that all such differences as we observe arise as a consequence of social conditioning.

There is an insidious temptation when talking about gender attributes to assume that the personality traits one treasures oneself are those that represent one's sex most adequately. The expectations and preferences of the opposite sex also play their part in deciding which qualities should be associated with gender. So generations of male writers romanticized the concept of 'woman' by imbuing it with all the qualities those men most wished to find in their mothers and wives, and women who needed to compensate for their undervalued position in society were happy to accept such positive value judgements. As a result, we heard a great deal about the gentleness, compassion, tenderness and patience of women, until in time these became recognized as typical feminine qualities.

There is no overwhelming evidence that women are by nature any more gentle, compassionate, tender or patient than men, though, because they are expected to be, they may try harder to accord to these ideals. By aspiring to measure up to an ideal of 'female virtue' during her formative years, a young girl may absorb certain behaviour patterns and emotional responses that then become part of her adult personality; but qualities adopted in this way are learned rather than innate. We are still a long way from being able to ascribe culture-free characteristics to the sexes. Any ideas we have about womanhood that correspond too closely with the 'ideal English lady' must be tested out against the legend of the Amazons, and the history and present-day experience of Chinese, Soviet or Eskimo women. Further, if we are honest, we will not be entirely happy to accept that just because we believe the Holy Spirit to be tender and patient, the Holy Spirit is therefore mother-like. Recent decades, in which we have at last started to liberate men, have seen thousands of wonderfully tender and patient young fathers introducing the next generation of infants to new facets of fatherhood.

The debate as to whether there really are some personality traits that are inherently feminine, in the sense that they are more likely to occur in women than in men, continues. The ideal of *androgyny* is explored by a number of feminist writers,[1] who believe this may free human beings to develop qualities that in the past have been seen as the preserve of the opposite sex. An androgynous person is one who has the qualities of both female and male, rather than, as in the case of an hermaphrodite, having neither. If God has all qualities, then God must be androgynous, but to ascribe androgyny to God does not imply that God is an hermaphrodite.[2]

Other feminist writers, however, see the concept of androgyny as fundamentally flawed, by continuing to define the two sets of characteristics which come together in an androgynous person in terms of masculine and feminine.[3] It is far from self-evident, in any case, that everyone should aim for androgyny. Many women are happy to accord to the feminine archetype and would exhibit that particular set of personality traits whether or not these were designated feminine, and many men would display what we call masculine qualities even if these were called feminine. Gender roles are only wrong if they are forced upon individuals against their will or nature. The important point is that everyone has the potential for any quality, and people should therefore be allowed to be themselves without having to accord to a predetermined set of characteristics in order to satisfy the sexual stereotyping of others.

Given the variety of meanings and functions bound up with the concept of femininity and masculinity, it is advisable in discussing these terms to differentiate between their use as biologically-related qualities and as socially-determined, and therefore merely contingent, labels. We should also recognize that the words are frequently used metaphorically. In the same way as someone can display religious fervour or missionary zeal without being in the least religious, so a man may display feminine gentleness without compromising his maleness. This particular activity or quality can be described more graphically by metaphorical reference to a specified group.

If 'feminine' qualities are not necessarily the preserve of women, then they are used metaphorically in describing women in exactly the same way as they are in describing men. The qualities are defined by reference to an initial group in which they were identified, but they are now used as metaphors to describe either women or men. If gender qualities are used as metaphors, then they can be possessed by either sex: a woman may betray 'paternalistic' attitudes, a man may 'mother' his family or colleagues.

Therefore, we cannot say that the Holy Spirit is feminine simply because she possesses qualities that we call feminine, for such qualities do not lead us to use the feminine pronoun, and a man may possess such qualities without being referred to as 'she'. In any case, we can also discover qualities of the Holy Spirit that would more appropriately be designated masculine. Nevertheless, in each age and culture many of the qualities popularly deemed to be feminine have been qualities that we identify and celebrate in the Holy Spirit. The ascription of femininity to these qualities may tell us more about that particular society's attitude to women than it does about God, but the very fact that such qualities have been designated feminine *and* been ascribed to the Holy Spirit, at least suggests that there is no innate contradiction in using metaphorically feminine qualities to describe the Holy Spirit.

LINGUISTIC GENDER

As well as being used to describe qualities and people, 'feminine' and 'masculine' are also used to define aspects of language. One of the questions we wish to investigate is whether it is reasonable to refer to the Holy Spirit in feminine terms, or, in other words, can we use the pronoun 'she' for the Holy Spirit?

English is not, of course, as dependent on gender as many other languages that are based on grammatical rather than natural gender, but we do still use words that are gender-specific. 'Waiter' and 'waitress' are, respectively, masculine and feminine words which describe the same occupation. 'Mother' and 'father', 'brother' and 'sister' are all gender-defining words, whereas the epicene alternatives of 'parent' and 'sibling' are not. There is dispute over whether some words should be epicene or gender-specific, for male chauvinism has in some cases assigned a lower value to the feminine equivalents of masculine terms. So, for instance, a female writer may be called a poet or an author, where these terms are treated as epicene, or a poetess or authoress, in which case she is distinguished from male writers, sometimes to her detriment. Because of this value-ascription, many women writers prefer not to use the feminine terms. The problem does not arise over the term 'novelist', which covers both male and female writers.

Although 'doctor' and 'nurse' are epicene words, because of the historical expectation that men are doctors and women are nurses, many people still qualify the words to make the one that does not accord with the stereotype gender-specific: so we have 'lady doctors' and 'male nurses'.[4] The problem of differing status also arises over whether ordained women should be called *priests*, since they follow the same profession as male priests, or *priestesses* because they are women. The first option overlooks any specific qualities they may bring to the work they do because they are women, while the second leaves room for chauvinist fear and discrimination.

To use words like 'she' or 'woman' is to use feminine language. But as well as referring to women, such feminine language can refer, metaphorically, to inanimate objects like boats or cars, which have no natural gender. In using such metaphors we imply both that the object has qualities that are traditionally called feminine, and also that our relationship with that object has something in common with our relationships with women as opposed to men.

Many women object to these metaphors, on the basis that they reflect undesirable attitudes to women, even when the properties are complimentary. For example, to ascribe the positive property of beauty to a car in terms that are normally used to describe a sexual liaison, can betray as negative an attitude to women as the derogatory property of being stubborn. Neither beauty nor stubbornness is truly feminine since both are, and have always been, just as much the preserve of men as of women. But both imply a relationship in which men have the same rights of ownership over women as they have over their cars, and therefore the relationship implied by the use of the metaphor can be offensive to women.

The feminine language that is used to describe the Church or one's native country reflects a different kind of relationship, this time with a mother or a chaste queen. The love and respect a man feels he owes his country is bound up with the love and respect he is expected to show to his mother. Although women do occasionally use feminine language to refer to cars, boats, a country or the Church, it is less common for them to do so, presumably because these metaphors do not spring out of the normal relationship they have with other women.

It would therefore be fair to say that in English we only use the feminine pronoun if the object is, literally or metaphorically, female. If it is literally female it has certain identifiable actual or potential sexual characteristics. If it is metaphorically female, we relate to it as though to a female, either because of certain qualities we detect in it that we commonly ascribe to females, or because we see it in the light of another relationship, such as wife, mother, daughter or queen.

Linguistic gender in theology

The reason why God has been referred to in the masculine gender for so long is not that he is a man, for God is not male or female. Nor is it because people have detected in God exclusively masculine qualities, for God lacks neither masculine nor feminine qualities. Instead, the reason lies in the choice of metaphors that have helped people to relate to God through history. So metaphors of kingship, which were meaningful to the Israelites from the time of David onwards, specified the attitude of obedience and awe that was thought to be the 'divine right' of God. Once the metaphor of kingship became accepted, it was natural to use the same masculine pronoun to refer to God the king as was used to refer to human kings.

After the writing of the New Testament the metaphor of father for God became the most common, and is still for many people the one with which they are most comfortable. If we use such a male metaphor, then it is not surprising that we use masculine language to refer to the one who bears this metaphor. It was natural that the Jews, from whom we have inherited our ways of speaking of God, should have used the masculine pronoun for the deity, for, living in a patriarchal culture, the metaphors they chose to describe God were predominantly based on important, and therefore male, people.

We can only speak of God in personal terms through metaphor and, as we have seen, our choice of metaphor to a great extent determines the language gender we use. While we cannot say that God the Holy Spirit is female, since God is male and female in perfect harmony, we may well find that a metaphor of femaleness, such as motherhood, is one that helps us to relate meaningfully to the Holy Spirit. Such a biologically related metaphor, unlike the socially determined qualities discussed earlier, would not simply be a reflection of our present attitudes to women, but would have something important to say about our understanding of God. I hope to show, in the next chapter, that this metaphor, which refers not just to the qualities but also to the activities of the Holy Spirit, is at least as powerful and useful as the metaphor of the fatherhood of God the Creator; and, with a proper understanding of the Holy Trinity, has the added advantage that it neither contradicts nor interferes with our use of that other much-loved metaphor.

CHAPTER SIX

The Feminine Face of God

Teach us to care and not to care
Teach us to sit still
Even among these rocks,
Our peace in his will
And even among these rocks
Sister, mother
And spirit of the river, spirit of the sea,
Suffer me not to be separated
And let my cry come unto Thee. [1]

We come, therefore, to the hypothesis that God the Holy Spirit can be perceived as and referred to in feminine terms; and that if we make an effort to envisage the femininity of the Holy Spirit, we shall open ourselves to a fuller vision of God. In Chapter 7 we shall examine some of the historical data that substantiate the claim that such a conception of the Holy Spirit is not entirely new; that it is, on the contrary, historically acceptable. But first we must enquire what we might mean by the ascription of femininity to the Spirit, whether such a change of terminology would adequately express what the Holy Spirit means to us, and whether it is possible to adapt our thinking and speaking sufficiently to incorporate such language use.

We can begin by recognizing that, taking a purely pragmatic approach, it is *possible* to speak of the Holy Spirit in feminine terms. Because we believe that God was incarnate in Jesus Christ, who was a man, we most naturally accord that incarnation of God masculine characteristics: Jesus had a male body. It is fallacious, though perhaps not particularly surprising, that the same characteristics should be extended to the being of God the Father, whom many have envisaged as an older version of Jesus. But there is no reason at all to refer to the Holy Spirit as male. That which is pure spirit can have no physical characteristics, and any masculinity or femininity we might ascribe to the Spirit must arise out of the *activity* of the Spirit, not out of association with the historical Jesus or projections on to the deity by a male-dominant society.

METAPHORS FOR GOD

The Old Testament is full of different metaphors through which human beings have struggled to express their experience of divinity. As society has changed, and with it our conception of God, some of the early Jewish metaphors for God, which suggested that he was a judge, a warrior or a mighty king, have worn a little thin for us. We now have to re-evaluate our metaphors to find the ones that best describe our relationship with the creator of the world. For some, the image of 'Lover' is successful in bringing out the passionate nature of God's love for us; others find that 'Friend' reverberates more by emphasizing the faithfulness and patience of God. For others, a more abstract concept such as 'Ground of our being' conjures up appropriate associations, and many who struggle against unjust regimes combine their material and spiritual hopes by addressing God as 'Liberator'.

God as 'Father'

Of course, Christians have for many centuries valued the ascription of Father to God. The idea had begun to evolve through the Old Testament prophets and was sanctified by being used by Jesus himself—though Christians have in general settled for the deferential distance of 'Father', rather than the childlike intimacy of Jesus' 'Abba'. For someone who has enjoyed a rich and fulfilling relationship with a human father, this can still be a powerful metaphor for the God who loves and cares for us, and whose friendship helps to define who we are and what we can become.

It is because it is so deeply embedded in our religious consciousness that we sometimes forget that we use 'father' metaphorically, not literally, of God. Our most-used prayer begins 'Our Father', and many of us use 'Father' as a normal means of address whenever we turn to the deity. But within our normal understanding of the term, God is not our father. A father is one who by a physical act sends sperm from his body to fertilize the egg of a female, thus enabling a child to develop. This does not accord with our notions of a divinely created universe. Not even in the most fundamentalist interpretation of the Adam and Eve story does God 'father' the first man and woman. And obviously, once the theory of evolution is introduced, the physical fatherhood of God becomes a nonsense.

If it is objected that the word 'father' is simply used to denote respect and close affection, in the same way that we speak of a 'spiritual father', then we have already passed into metaphorical usage. Yes, of course God is like a father, which is why the term has always been so useful, but God is not a father as such. God is spirit, and those who worship him must worship him in spirit and in truth. God is *like* a father in that without him we would not exist, he loves us, we owe him love, respect and obedience, and he provides for us by creating us within a universe in which there is space and food for all—if we would but learn to share it. But God is also *like* a mother, and many people are now also exploring the potential of the metaphor 'mother' for God, and through this finding it possible to grow into a deeper relationship with the One from whom we come, and who we believe loves us deeply and tenderly.

In this age, when we are at last beginning to redress the balance between the sexes, it is important not to idealize the concept of motherhood. 'Mother' will conjure up for some people negative images of possessiveness, over-anxiousness, emotional manipulation and claustrophobic boredom. Obviously, these associations are no more helpful to our understanding of God than the equivalent associations that some people have of fatherhood: drunkenness, violence, absentee-ism or promiscuity. When we speak of the motherhood or fatherhood of God we are exploring ways in which the deepest relationships that humans experience can, *at their best*, light up our understanding of the divine nature and of our relationship with God.

God as 'Mother'

The image of God our mother is perhaps most potent for those privileged to have experienced motherhood themselves: giving birth, sustaining through feeding, suffering in and for a helpless infant too young to understand gratitude. The wonder of this experience may last only hours, or it may continue for a number of years, but while it lasts, it can bring unique insights into our relationship with God. My own experience of mothering certainly gave me a better understanding of that love which is self-giving not because it chooses to be, or because it is good to be, but because that is its *essence*. This insight has enabled me to respond to God my mother with renewed love and trust.

But whereas the experience of mothering applies primarily to those who have given birth, all of us, male and female, have some experience of being mothered. Whatever we may later have made of our relationship with our mother, there was a time when our whole being turned instinctively to that one person, expecting to receive love and nourishment. For most of us, our earliest experience of life is of being entirely and uniquely loved, and this we are able to take blissfully for granted in a way that we rarely, if ever, do again. This is a good place to start in our relationship with God because it grounds us in love and encourages us to develop an awareness that we are first, and for ever, loved by God our Mother.

God as 'Mother-Father'

The insights that come from the revelation that God is as much our mother as our father can be enriching and liberating, but they also raise some practical difficulties that we cannot ignore. For the context within which we learn our faith and engage in worship is one in which God has predominantly been perceived and addressed as male, and our whole language structure reflects this bias. To attempt to substitute feminine language for masculine runs the risk of self-consciousness and, what is worse, assumes that God must now be perceived as female rather than as the fullness of female and male together.

As was suggested in Chapter 2, much of the maleness of our 'God-talk' can be neutralized, and the Church certainly has a duty towards women to set this high on the agenda for the next few years. But if we try to wipe out all the masculine imagery that we have inherited, we are going to find our stock of images sadly depleted. Can we no longer pray the Lord's Prayer because it addresses God as father? Should we, in fact, abandon the ascription of lord to God completely? Must we reject all those parts of the Bible in which God is addressed in the masculine gender?

Radical feminists would indeed insist that our whole concept of God must be purged and, in so far as they are taking a bleak and stony path in which familiar metaphors and endearments for God are not available to them, we owe them a debt of gratitude for the service they are rendering to the language of theology. As with some of the theologians of liberation, these thinkers are working on behalf of all of us as they stretch our shrunken concept of God and help to develop a religious language more worthy of its theme. But the personal cost is high, and prophets are often lonely people.

The disadvantage of taking such a strong line, though, is that one is robbed of so much of the history and cultural background of Christianity. While we must live in the present and work for the coming of the Kingdom, much of the richness and strength of our corporate faith derives from history and tradition. There is therefore value in redeeming our chauvinist past, as well as in working for justice in the present.

If we hold on to our history, allowing the light of continuing scholarship and revelation to shine upon it, we are more likely to grow in understanding than if we simply reject the past because we have out-grown it. For example, we no longer see God in such anthropomorphic terms as some of our forebears did. But it is quite legitimate for us to accept a picture of God the father as the limit of human understanding in biblical times, and to appreciate the implications of this revelation for our personal relationship with God, even though we have moved on to a deeper understanding of God as Spirit. Metaphors are for using, for playing with, for helping us to enlarge our understanding and our emotional response. There is therefore no reason why the metaphor of God as father should not remain alive and vibrant, so long as we maintain an openness to the fresh truths revealed to us in new and different metaphors.

FEMININE AND MASCULINE WITHIN A LOVING GOD

In Chapter 3 the doctrine of the Trinity was described as, among other things, an attempt to concentrate our minds on the loving community within the heart of God. God, we believe, is the source of all our loving, is perfect love. But it is arguable that for such a relationship of love to flower, femininity must be included within the Trinity; otherwise, we shall have to concede that homosexuality is at the heart of our image of God. If, in exploring the ground of our being, the creator of the world, and the pattern of what life is all about, we are limited to three male 'persons' loving each other with no need for any female contribution, then we have got it all wrong about the union of male and female being the finest flowering of human love. For such a picture of co-habitation within an all-male community does not accord with our normal view of ideal love. In view of this, it is amusing to conjecture that many of those who would most resist any ascription of femininity to God would probably be the least tolerant of human homosexuality.

There is no doubt that many homosexuals enjoy beautiful and fulfilling relationships with members of their own sex, but it should also be recognized that traditionally our concept of love has had something to do with the complementarity of opposites. This applies particularly to the sexual act, where the opposites of male and female become one flesh. Although in an infinitely complex world we have to accommodate variations and deviations from the norm, this is still what our understanding of the nature of love is based upon.

If we viewed God solely as a repository of justice we could envisage a bench of male judges; a picture of the omnipotence of God might take the form of a cohort of soldiers, or one mighty warrior; but a picture of God as supreme love must incorporate both female and male. Given the implicit masculinity of the words 'Father' and 'Son', there is a case to be made, purely by elimination, for referring to the Holy Spirit in feminine terms. So one reason for ascribing femininity to the Holy Spirit relates to our understanding of God as love. For God to be understood as a loving harmonious community of persons, femininity must be present within the Godhead.

Now what we really believe, or certainly should believe, is that all of God is both male and female, that our father God is also our mother and that Jesus Christ the Son is no less an exemplar of feminine virtues than masculine ones. Nevertheless, we have seen that it is extremely difficult to retain the words 'father' and 'son' to describe God without succumbing to a limiting of our view of that God in a masculine light. To ascribe femininity to the Holy Spirit, as long as we come to a proper understanding of the divinity of the Holy Spirit, enables us to use the feminine gender in referring to God without having to alter our traditional trinitarian terminology.

Some would argue that it is high time that we did change our terminology, since to use such words as 'father' and 'son' to describe the divinity is dangerously misleading. While this position carries some weight, I think it does not accord adequate recognition of two facts.

First, it overlooks the fact that rather than being entirely negative, 'father' and 'son' have been extremely rich and useful metaphors for expressing what we have come to understand of God. The only pity is that we have become so comfortable with these particular terms that we have failed to explore other, equally rich and useful, metaphors that might have given us a deeper appreciation of some of the more feminine aspects of God. Secondly, and more practically, to change the basic terminology that we use to talk about God is an enormous undertaking, requiring the consent and co-operation of millions of Christians throughout the world. It would require us to provide new metaphors which were as potentially valuable and universal, and to teach people, in scores of different languages, to adopt our revised terminology.

This is not the case with the ascription of femininity to the Holy Spirit. As we shall see in Chapter 7, several of the languages most commonly used for 'God-talk' in history denote the Spirit in linguistically feminine words, and for those of us who do not speak such tongues, a very slight shift is required before we start to use 'she' of the Holy Spirit, and the traditional formulation of the Trinity can be left absolutely unaffected.

It has already been established that maleness and femaleness describe physical characteristics that relate to potential biological function. In this literal sense, it is clearly vacuous to ascribe maleness to God for, even in the anthropomorphism of some of the ancient writings, God does not sport a penis or engage in sexual activity. This, in fact, is one of the features that distinguishes our concept of God from that of Hindus or the ancient Greeks, where the erotic nature of divinity is celebrated.

Mary Hayter[2] has suggested that it was a desire to distance themselves from those religions in which God was a begetter that was responsible for the infrequency with which the term 'Father' was used for God in the Old Testament, where it occurs only fifteen times, as opposed to the 245 times in which God is referred to as 'Father' in the New Testament. For Jews and Christians, the creation of life came about by the pronouncement of the Word rather than through the reproductive cycle. Once one comes to the revelation that God is Spirit, then maleness and femaleness have no meaning at all. Since it is only maleness or femaleness that determine whether someone should be referred to as 'he' or 'she', it is clear that the general referent 'he' for God is gravely misleading.

Nevertheless, if we found that our knowledge of God consistently presented us with a being with exclusively masculine qualities, this might incline us towards the adoption of masculine language to refer to the deity on the basis that 'he' was at least more male than female. But whether we understand 'feminine' and 'masculine' in terms of social expectation, or personality traits derivative of hormonal activity, or as biologically related metaphors, God cannot be defined as masculine.

Several of the biblical writers were at pains to point out that God had feminine as well as masculine qualities, for a God who is perfect should not lack any qualities. Thus as early as the writing of the Pentateuch, God was described in terms that accord more closely to a traditional feminine ideal than a masculine one: 'Yahweh, Yahweh, a God of tenderness and compassion, slow to anger, rich in kindness and faithfulness.'[3] By the time we come to the rich poetry of the Book of Isaiah, such qualities are in astonishing profusion. So we read that God is one who is vulnerable to suffering, who pleads and reasons, who takes people by the hand to guide and reassure them, who longs to console and heal, whose prominent qualities are pity, gentleness, patience and long-suffering—qualities which, at that time and in that culture, were seen as feminine. 'For I, Yahweh, your God, I am holding you by the right hand; I tell you, "Do not be afraid, I will help you";'[4] And, '. . . for the mountains may depart, the hills be shaken, but my love for you will never leave you and my covenant of peace with you will never be shaken, says Yahweh who takes pity on you';[5] Also, 'Like a son comforted by his mother will I comfort you.'[6]

However, as we have seen, the possession of these particular qualities does not imply that the subject is female, and many a traditionalist would claim that God happens to be a male who exemplifies feminine qualities as well as masculine ones. But on the basis that feminine qualities do not make people female, the possession of masculine ones does not make them male either. So, on the one hand, it is not true that God only possesses masculine characteristics; on the other, even if this *were* seen to be true, that would still not mean that God was male and should be referred to in the masculine gender.

If, however, the masculinity of God is confined to biologically related characteristics, then, as we saw in Chapter 5, the only quality we would be able to ascribe to God with any conviction would be aggression. Far from being happy with this conclusion, most people would probably prefer to ascribe to God the biologically feminine quality of maternity. But, in both these cases, there are no physical features to which the qualities can refer back, since God possesses neither testosterone nor womb, so again they are of little use in describing a God whom we believe to be spiritual rather than physical.

Therefore, the only use of the terms 'feminine' and 'masculine' that we can meaningfully apply to God is the *metaphorical* use, and, as we have already seen, those metaphors that relate to fatherhood are often apposite in defining our relationship with God. In the same way as the qualities of providing for us, directing us, or chiding us stem directly from the metaphor of human fatherhood, so there is a whole nest of qualities of God that stem from a similar metaphor of motherhood and should lead us to call God our mother; and these qualities are celebrated by the Old Testament writers as much as the qualities that could be seen as metaphors for fatherhood. Thus God is likened to a midwife, a mother and a mistress, as well as a master in the Psalms (22.9; 131.2; 123.2), and female images for God in Isaiah include a pregnant woman and a nursing mother (42.14; 66.13).

It is an essential element of a metaphor that it is not, literally, that which it lays claim to be, but that by creating an analogy it can shed new light on something with which we are familiar. If this is true of the feminine images of God, it is also true of the masculine ones. As G. W. H. Lampe has argued: ' "Father" is an analogy which illuminates basic aspects of God's dealings with us; but it does not mean that God is literally a father, a masculine person.'[7]

The fact that the metaphor of the motherhood of God is useful and is likely to gain currency as women are accorded more respect in society, does not diminish the linguistic difficulties that arise over referring to God as both mother and father, 'she' and 'he'. I have pointed out that the sexual connotations of using the terms 'father' and 'son' make it easier to refer to these aspects of God in the masculine gender, whereas the Holy Spirit is not limited by such masculine imagery.

THE MOTHERHOOD OF THE SPIRIT

Motherhood is a much more apposite metaphor for our relationship with the Holy Spirit. In the Bible this Spirit is frequently associated with birth; at creation with the hatching of the 'egg' of the world; at the annunciation, with the promise of the 'second creation', God incarnate; and at Pentecost, with the birth of the Christian Church. Further, many of the particular qualities that we ascribe to God the Holy Spirit are those that we regard as feminine, either because they correspond to the expectations and prejudices of our society or because they conform to the biologically related metaphors for God—particularly those of motherhood.

Many women never give birth to children, and they are no less womanly for that, any more than a man is lacking in manliness until he has fathered children. Nevertheless, it is the potential for physically mothering and fathering infants that uniquely defines whether we are male or female. Thus, when searching for an adequate metaphor for the Holy Spirit, we should examine how appropriate to our understanding of God are the qualities that stem directly from our differentiating physical characteristics. Let us therefore look at some of the strictly biological functions of motherhood to see how they relate metaphorically to God the Holy Spirit.

The first undeniable feature of motherhood is the ability to conceive, for new life to come into being. The ovum is in the woman's body throughout her life, but when it is fertilized it begins to grow and becomes life in its own right: 'In the beginning was the Word, and the Word was with God.'[8] Or, as Julian of Norwich expressed it, 'We owe our being to him—and this is the essence of motherhood.'[9]

It is the Holy Spirit who effects creation, bringing life to birth. For at the dawn of time, according to the first verse of Genesis, it was the Spirit of God who hovered over the waters, and this creative function has continued throughout history: 'Thou shalt send forth thy Spirit and they shall be created.'[10] The creation of life, of bringing to birth, is a feminine activity, a biologically related metaphor. In the same way as the incarnation could only come through a woman, so that Mary was necessary for the birth of God, so the birth of creation implies a mother. If we believe that it is the Holy Spirit of God who is responsible for creation, then it is reasonable to ascribe femininity to that Holy Spirit. From this Holy Spirit, our Mother, we all come.

Next, a mother bears the child in her womb for nine months. During that time the child is growing into an individual person, with unique characteristics, and yet is one with the mother and receives all from her and lives only through her: 'In God we live and move and have our being.'[11] If we live in God we live in the Spirit, and that Spirit is the One who sustains us.

By giving birth and cutting the umbilical cord, the mother, while still loving as much as—if not more than—before, separates the child from herself for its own good, gives it identity. God sets us free to be ourselves but, like a mother, continues to protect and nourish us, to feed us with whatever we need: 'Hide me under the shadow of thy wing.'[12] This guiding, protecting and inspiring are ways in which all Christians can know the presence of the Holy Spirit in their lives as she continues to fulfil this maternal role.

But, above all, the relationship of a mother with her unborn or newly born child is nearly always one of love, in which the needs of the child will be of paramount importance to the mother. Even though there are exceptional cases where this love does not materialize, the reaction appears to be an entirely natural response to the process of giving birth. It is therefore a particularly appropriate metaphor for God's love for us, and should teach us to value ourselves in the same way as a well-mothered child growing up in a happy family develops self-esteem. Also, in the same way as a good mother frees her child to respond openly and courageously to life, so our awareness of the motherhood of God can free us to come to terms with the reality of life, to respond positively to a world created in love, and to offer respect and compassion to the people we meet in this joyful and suffering world.

It is through the Holy Spirit that we experience and share the love of

God and, as most people begin to learn the art of loving from their human mothers, so we, 'being rooted and grounded in love',[13] grow spiritually in this love by being fed by the Spirit. As we mature, so we discover that we are constantly presented with the option of adopting or rejecting this life of love in the Spirit.

The symbolism of birth is preserved by the Church in the sacrament of baptism, through which we enter into life in the Spirit. Whether we do it literally by total immersion or by the token gesture of water poured over the head, we symbolically enter into the pre-natal waters before emerging from the womb into new life. As we shall see in Chapter 7, this emphasis was clearly preserved in some of the Syrian baptismal rites, and the association of water, birth and the Holy Spirit is one that both ancient myth and twentieth-century dynamic psychology would understand as leading to a perception of the Holy Spirit as a mother.

It is in the story of Christ's baptism in the Jordan that we are first made aware of his relationship with God the Spirit. As Jesus emerges from the water, leaving his early years behind and being spiritually reborn, the Holy Spirit appears as a dove and the voice of God is heard. At this moment Jesus is given reassurance of his Sonship with a force and clarity that he rarely seems to have experienced again. It is as though at the start of his new life he is granted the privilege accorded to most ordinary babies in their first days of life. He knows himself to be loved and valued as a child in the arms of his mother.

But, as well as this strong biologically related metaphor for the Holy Spirit, we can also take cognisance of the weaker, socially determined gender attributes. If there is an assumption in our society that such activities and qualities as nourishing, tenderness, compassion, and patience are associated with femininity, then we reflect the reality of our life within society when we infer from the presence of these qualities in the Holy Spirit that the Holy Spirit is feminine. The image evoked, for instance, by Gerard Manley Hopkins in some of his poetry, is of a Holy Spirit who, within the norms and assumptions of Western Christendom, is feminine, who broods and coos like a dove and who even has a comforting warm female breast:

> And for all this, nature is never spent;
>   There lives the dearest freshness deep down things;
> And though the last lights off the black West went
>   Oh, morning, at the brown brink eastward, springs—
> Because the Holy Ghost over the bent
>   World broods with warm breast and with ah! bright wings.[14]

The hovering, sheltering and protecting aspects of the Holy Spirit have also been seen as feminine attributes and, as we shall see in Chapter 7, this aspect appears in the feminine concept of the Shekinah. So the Holy Spirit is female in terms of metaphorical procreation and also feminine in terms of the present assumptions of society. Since I am not asserting the exclusive femaleness of God the Holy Spirit we can also, of course, recognize that the Spirit has male and masculine elements, so that she is at times seen as the one who makes pregnant and who inspires.

Finally, the assumption of the dove as the symbol of the Holy Spirit, which gradually entered the iconography of the Christian Church, adds weight to the choice of a female personification of the Holy Spirit. For not only is the dove seen as a gentle creature and gentleness culturally ascribed to the female, but the dove is also an appropriate symbol for motherhood as we understand it. For by prolaction pigeons and doves produce in their bodies a soft white substance, known as pigeon's milk, which is passed from the mouth of the adult bird into the mouth of the young. Among all birds, therefore, it is closest to our ideal of motherhood.

Christian feminists such as Rosemary Radford Ruether would wish to move right away from the image of both father *and* mother for God, since they feel that such picture-language allows us to avoid coming of age and relating to God as mature adults.[15] But the fact that the Holy Spirit possesses maternal qualities does not limit her solely to those, any more than our human mothers are restricted to the mothering actions and instincts upon which we depended in infancy. As we grow into adulthood our mothers often become our friends, and a mother who refused to allow her children to grow up and relate to her as mature adults would almost certainly forfeit the love and respect of those children. So seeing the Holy Spirit as a mother should not limit us to a conception of God as Creator. In the same way as our human mothers become our friends without ceasing to be mothers, so we can celebrate God the Holy Spirit as Sustainer and Liberator without denying her motherhood.

The issue of the gender we use to refer to the Holy Spirit is not just a feminist issue. It is not concerned with equity between women and men, important as that is, but with our very conception of the nature of God. If it were simply a matter of sharing out divinity betweeen the sexes, making part of God male and part female, we would be creating God in our own image. On the contrary, it is because *we* are created in the image of *God*, both female and male bearing the imprint of the Creator, that we must strive to preserve the undifferentiated harmony of God. 'God created man in the image of himself, in the image of God he created him, male and female he created them.'[16] As Yves Congar reflected in referring to this verse, 'If this is true, then there must be in God, in a transcendent form, something that corresponds to masculinity and something that corresponds to femininity.'[17] By allowing us to celebrate the perfect wholeness and loving communion of God, rather than pandering to a lop-sided male idol, this might help all men and women to delight in and develop their feminine qualities and thus grow into more whole human beings.

In order to expand our vision of God beyond the artificial boundaries of gender that constrict the lives of human beings, there is no need for us to invent new symbols, or to expand on the doctrine of the Trinity. For the wholeness that we seek, the unity of feminine and masculine in God, is there, in the Trinity and in our oldest understanding of the Holy Spirit. We have only missed it because we tried to masculinize the Holy Spirit. But the feminine is there, both in terms of activity and in terms of qualities, right at the heart of God.

CHAPTER SEVEN

World-Mothering Air

Be thou, then, O thou dear
Mother, my atmosphere;
My happier world, wherein
To wend and meet no sin;

. . . Stir in my ears, speak there
Of God's love, O live air,
Of patience, penance, prayer:
World-mothering air, air wild,
Wound with thee, in thee isled,
Fold home, fast fold thy child. [1]

If an interpretation of the Spirit of God as feminine were applicable only to women living in the Western world, it would be of local interest to sociologists of religion and might even affect the prayer life of a number of individuals, but would not clarify humanity's vision of God or help the Church to live more fully in the Spirit in God's world. For that, it must also, at least in theory, be meaningful to the Pope and the Archbishop of Canterbury, to the Russian Orthodox worshipper and to the recent convert to Christianity in an African village. Such universality would be difficult to achieve if the thesis were incompatible with the historical records of human understanding of the transcendent that we all share in our Scriptures. To these Scriptures we now turn; for, as we shall find, rather than being an invention of the twentieth century, the conception of the Spirit of God in feminine terms is, in fact, grounded in our most ancient biblical records.

Evidence from the past does not, of course, mean that we should accept the femininity of the Holy Spirit without question, for that which is old is not necessarily true. I believe that mistakes have always arisen from our limited knowledge and vision and that God is continually being revealed throughout history, enabling us to grow in understanding.

Sometimes, however, new revelation allows us to look back and see a pattern emerging in the past that we could not decipher before. The stranger who talked to Cleopas and his friend on the Emmaus road took them back over the Scriptures that they knew well, to help them to see the truth they had missed: that it was part of the essential nature of things that the Messiah should suffer. Their revelation in the present cast light back on the past. Similarly, once we have encountered the idea that the Holy Spirit can be described in feminine terms, we may look back and find precedents for such an interpretation throughout the Bible and Church history.

LINGUISTIC GENDER IN THE BIBLE

The authenticity of the use of feminine words to denote the Holy Spirit is deeply rooted in the Old Testament, for the Hebrew word that we translate as Spirit is *ruah*, which is feminine in form and grammatical use.[2] So before the world was and God's Spirit prepared to bring the chaos into a harmony, it was 'she' who hovered over the waters 'like a bird hanging in the air over its young in the nest'.[3] Similarly, when God entered the prophets, causing them to speak out and effect change in the world, it was, grammatically, the feminine spirit that was the manifestation of God's activity and presence.[4]

It would be unwise to place too much weight on this linguistic peculiarity. The ascription of the feminine gender to the word denoting spirit did not, of course, mean that the Hebrews believed that the Spirit of God, or any other spirit, was female. The French language today still requires that any small wailing human being should be referred to as *le bébé*, yet no one doubts that about half the babies born in France will grow into little girls. But, as we observed in Chapter 2, the language we use does affect the way we view things, and when we meet *un bébé* we can experience difficulties in relating to it until we know whether it is a baby girl or a baby boy. Should we, for instance, comment on how pretty and endearing the child is, or how big and strong?

For another example of the way in which our language influences our thought, one may look at *mater*, the Latin word for mother, and see how, by springing from this etymological root, the material world came to be seen as feminine. On the one hand, this gave us the anthropomorphic concept of Mother Nature, with its associated images of rhythm, fecundity and birth-giving; on the other hand, it allowed the early Church Fathers to drive a wedge between the material and spiritual worlds, associating the material with the feminine and the spiritual with the masculine, thus entrenching the belief that women were part of the evil in the world which was preventing men from achieving spiritual perfection.

While the fact that the Spirit is referred to throughout the Old Testament in the feminine gender proves nothing in terms of what

gender that Spirit might actually be, it did diminish the risk of the
Hebrews conceiving of the Spirit of God in purely masculine terms. So
Elijah was able to hear the Spirit speaking to him in a 'still small voice',
and Zechariah came to understand that mighty acts of God could come
about through other means than those associated with masculine force:
'Not by might, nor by power, but by my spirit, saith the Lord of hosts.'
It would be begging the question to claim that these instances represent
the femininity of the Spirit, but they do at least introduce images that
do not accord with a macho deity. The Aramaic spoken by Jesus and his
disciples is closely related to Hebrew, and so the culture in which Jesus
was embedded was one in which a feminine word was used to denote the
Spirit of God, both in the Scriptures and in normal everyday speech.

With the writing of the New Testament in Greek we have the
introduction of a different language base with which to build our
concepts of God. The Greek word for spirit which is used in the New
Testament is a neuter word *pneuma* which, one may feel, at least leaves
the question of gender open. No one could claim that the New
Testament writers were indifferent to the Holy Spirit. The word
pneuma occurs 375 times in the New Testament, and, as in the Old
Testament, covers a number of related but not identical ideas,
including divine guidance, the presence of God, and the promptings of
personal conscience. It was only by a gradual process of hypostasi-
zation, completed in the post-canonical writings, that the Spirit moved
definitively away from representing an aspect or activity of God, such as
breath, to become a more uniquely personal entity, or a *person*, within
the Godhead.

A neuter word is not ideal for denoting a person, particularly a divine
person, and when St John wanted to suggest that the coming of the
Holy Spirit on the disciples would give them the experience of being in
relationship, he felt driven to introduce a new word to describe this
spirit, *parakletos*. Although we translate the Paraclete as 'Comforter', a
word that for most people evokes images of femininity, the Greek word
is in fact masculine. Since the word occurs when Jesus is reassuring his
disciples that another will come to take his place when he leaves, it is
appropriate that a masculine form of denotation should here be used.

As I have stressed, the Holy Spirit is no more intrinsically feminine
than God is masculine. What is at issue is the language which we may
legitimately use to describe our experience of God, the Holy Spirit.
Disciples, filled with foreboding as it dawns on them that they are to
lose that person who has become for them the very presence of God in
their lives, might well have needed a concept of the Holy Spirit which
was as close to their experience of Jesus as it was possible for spirit to be
to a man. It is noteworthy, therefore, that what Jesus promises is that
God will send *another* Paraclete. As Jesus has comforted and
strengthened his disciples over the past few years, so will another come

to fulfil this function in the disciples' lives. Jesus does not say that this is all that the Holy Spirit will do, but that this is at least one role the Holy Spirit will perform.

The normal word for spirit in the New Testament Greek, then, is *pneuma*, a neuter word, but when the Bible was translated into Latin the masculine word, *spiritus*, was chosen to bear the meaning of *ruah* and *pneuma*. Various other words could have been used, including a feminine word such as *anima*. This Latin word has both a masculine form, *animus*, and a feminine form, *anima*, and it is interesting to note how the two words diverged in connotation, with the animus becoming associated with the mind, and the anima with the soul. While this, again, facilitates a sexual differentiation whereby the masculine is accorded more respect than the feminine—in this case by being more closely identified with the intellect—it is certainly arguable that the anima would more accurately represent the Holy Spirit to us, as the soul, or very being, of God.

So it was that when Jesus used the word *spirit* in his native Aramaic he used a feminine word; when it was translated into Greek for general readership it took the form of a neuter noun and later, when Latin became the universal language of the Church, the masculine term *spiritus* took its place. In this masculine form it was more easily assimilated into what was increasingly perceived as a male God, and our concept of God lost the wholeness that it might have been able to retain if theology had continued to be undertaken in a language like Hebrew, which referred to God's spirit in the feminine gender.

CONCEPTS OF SPIRIT IN THE EARLY CHURCH

Latin, however, was not the only language of the early Church, for the churches that grew in the countries bordering the eastern Mediterranean continued to use the Syriac language which was close to the Aramaic used by Jesus and his associates, and thus related to Hebrew. In this language several of the early theologians explored the mystery of God and developed their own ways of understanding the material to which they, too, were heirs. So, although the New Testament itself entered the Syrian Church in the Greek language, it was understood within an essentially Semitic frame of reference. The early Syrian Church also assimilated a good deal of other material, written in Syriac, which was never translated into Greek and which helped to form the particular texture of poetry and faith which has only begun to receive its deserved attention in recent years.

Therefore, although the feminine form was lost to the Western Church when it came under the influence of Rome, the Church that grew up in Syria continued for several centuries to refer to the Holy Spirit using a feminine noun, *ruha d-qudsha*, meaning 'spirit of holiness'. If it is true that the language we use is bound to influence the concepts we form, then it is not very surprising that this Syrian Church, which, at least initially, used the feminine gender to denote the Holy Spirit, was able to maintain a view of that Spirit which was wide enough to embrace the analogy of motherhood. For example, although very little remains of the Gospel according to the Hebrews, one of the fragments we have of this work describes Jesus Christ referring to the Holy Spirit as his mother: 'Even so did my mother, the Holy Spirit, take me by one of my hairs and carry me away on a great mountain of Tabor.'[5] Aphrahat, too, uses similar terminology with no hint of an apology for ascribing motherhood to the Holy Spirit: 'As long as a man has not taken a wife, he loves and reveres God his Father and the Holy Spirit his Mother, and he has no other love. But when a man takes a wife, then he leaves his (true) Father and Mother.'[6]

Sebastian Brock, in his study of the Syrian baptismal tradition, also records a strange detail about the Acts of Thomas. In one of the prayers of Judas Thomas, in which he invokes the Holy Spirit, we find, in the Greek version, the words 'Come, compassionate Mother'. This Greek text is a translation of an earlier Syriac text, yet in the Syriac version that has come down to us this phrase is missing. It would appear that later editors of the Acts of Thomas considered the ascription of motherhood to the Holy Spirit to be suspect and therefore dropped it, but it did not occur to anyone to expurgate the Greek translation.

The metaphor of the Holy Spirit as our mother is strengthened by the imagery surrounding baptism, in which one goes once more into the waters in order to be reborn in the Spirit. According to John's Gospel, Jesus told Nicodemus that he must be born again. When Nicodemus questioned the practicality of this recommendation, Jesus went on to explain his figure of speech in terms of entering a new life in the Spirit through baptism:

> I tell you most solemnly,
> unless a man is born through water and the Spirit,
> he cannot enter the kingdom of God:
> What is born of the flesh is flesh;
> what is born of the Spirit is spirit.[7]

In this discussion, where the entrance into new life is compared with physical birth, Jesus finds no problem in using the analogy of motherhood for the Holy Spirit. This symbolism of water and birth is retained with particular force in the Syrian tradition, where the womb of baptism figures in the baptismal liturgies:

> Instead of the womb of Eve which produced children who were mortal and corruptible, may this womb of water produce children who are heavenly, spiritual and immortal; and as the Holy Spirit

hovered over the water at the establishment of created things, do you, O Lord, be present in this baptismal water, which is the spiritual womb that gives birth to spiritual beings; and may it produce, instead of the Adam made of dust, the heavenly Adam.[8]

Under the continuing Greek influence, *ruha* came, from about the fifth century onwards, to take on a masculine connotation when applied to the third person of the Trinity. However, although the major examples of feminine pneumatic terminology occur in the first four centuries A.D., there are a few much later examples, particularly in relation to the Spirit's action of hovering, which continued to be seen as an essentially feminine activity. Sahdona (c. 600) refers to the Holy Spirit hovering like a mother as she santifies, and some 300 years later Moshe bar Kepha describes how the Holy Spirit 'hovered over John the Baptist and brought him up like a compassionate mother'.[9]

Although awareness of the Holy Spirit as feminine is not generally apparent in the New Testament canonical writings, there is reason to believe that such ascription was more widespread than our tradition would indicate. Several of the manuscripts found at Nag Hammadi in 1945, for instance, which record some of the Gnostic writings from these centuries, suggest that there was nothing very unusual at that time in ascribing femininity to God the Holy Spirit. In both the Gospel to the Hebrews and the Gospel of Thomas we find Jesus referring to his mother the Holy Spirit, and the Apocryphon of John describes a vision of the Holy Trinity in which the Holy Spirit appears as mother with God the Father and the Son. The familiarity of this family-style version of a trinity in pagan religions would have militated against its being embraced by the early Church in the same way as the early Jews, when carving out their religious identity, were extremely nervous about feminine imagery for God because of the fertility rites and goddess worship that they witnessed in the religions from which they wanted to dissociate themselves.

But the ascription of motherhood to the Holy Spirit was sufficiently uncontroversial for it to appear, in the Coptic Gospel of Philip, as a premise in an argument concerning the virgin birth: 'Some have said that Mary conceived of the Holy Spirit. They are wrong, and they do not realize what they are saying, for when did a woman ever conceive of a woman?'[10] Instead of arguing, as he might well have tried to do, from the fact of the virgin birth to the impossibility of ascribing femininity to the Holy Spirit, the writer uses the fact of the Spirit's femininity to argue that the virgin birth should not therefore be interpreted too literally in physical terms. He does this by claiming that what the passage means is not that Mary conceived without the involvement of Joseph, but that the conception of Jesus represents the union of two divine powers, God the Father and the Holy Spirit the Mother.

Not only did the Gnostic sects retain an element of maternal femininity within their conception of God, but some of them even accorded women an equal status with men in their churches, accepting them as fellow-workers in Christ. In such sects, the inclusion of women in the most sacred parts of worship was seen not only as just, but as in accordance with Jesus' treatment of such friends as Mary Magdalene. As Gnosticism lost ground to orthodoxy, and the Church settled into a respectability more in tune with the current mores of society, such irregular behaviour became outlawed by a Church that was increasingly dominated by a male hierarchical clergy, and theological thinking became ever more deeply coloured by maleness.

WISDOM

But *ruah* is not the only model from which our understanding of the Holy Spirit was to develop. Later in the Old Testament, and initially bearing a strong resemblance to the philosophies of the nations surrounding Israel, we have the development of the Wisdom literature. In its earliest and simplest form this literature offers short pithy sayings (*meshalim*), such as we find in Proverbs: sayings that could be easily memorized and passed on orally from one generation to the next.

As it developed, this literary form was used to thrash out some of the intractable questions of philosophy, such as the problem of suffering. In the earlier Wisdom books, for instance, the belief is expressed that suffering only falls on the wicked to punish them for their misdeeds, while the good will be rewarded with happiness. By the time the books of Job and Ecclesiastes were written, however, it had dawned on the thinkers of the day that this rather facile equation does not adequately accord with the facts, and they began to explore a theology that takes more account of the suffering of the good and innocent.

The thinkers from these different Middle Eastern cultures were all seeking for what they called 'Wisdom'. Wisdom appears to have represented for them that which is true and good, that which is the meaning behind the apparent order of the world, that which was eternal rather than temporal. In other words, it represented their religious quest and, in so far as they found what they were seeking, it would be fair to say that they came at least to a partial vision of the nature of God. As the culture became more influenced by Greek thought and language, Wisdom took on an aura of the transcendent. At the same time it also became more embedded in the Jewish religion and so Wisdom naturally became closely associated with the Hebrew idea of God, so paving the way for the later Christian attempts to perceive God in different aspects. 'From everlasting I was firmly set, from the beginning, before earth came into being.'[11] And, 'Although alone, she can do all; herself unchanging, she makes all things new.'[12]

So Wisdom was personified, and was personified not as a man or a god, but as a woman. This literature therefore developed one aspect of the feminine principle of God's creative energy, or what we would normally call the Holy Spirit of God.

> And so I prayed, and understanding was given me;
> I entreated, and the spirit of Wisdom came to me,
> I esteemed her more than sceptres and thrones;
> compared with her, all gold is a pinch of sand,
> and beside her silver ranks as mud.
> I loved her more than health or beauty,
> preferred her to the light, since her radiance never sleeps.
> In her company all good things came to me,
> at her hands riches not to be numbered.
> All these I delighted in, since Wisdom brings them,
> but as yet I did not know she was their mother.[13]

The creative energy of God is seen in the process of history, and beginning at the tenth chapter of Wisdom the writer traces the history of the Jews, showing the divine guidance of Wisdom as the action of God among people. This action, again, accords closely with what we would understand to be the Spirit of God working in the world.

It is therefore possible to assimilate the figure of Wisdom recorded in the Old Testament with the Spirit of God to which later, Christian, writings ascribe divinity as the third person of the Trinity. It is noteworthy, in this connection, that the psalmist on occasion appears to equate Wisdom with the Spirit of God. So, in Psalm 104, when the psalmist is celebrating the wonders of the created world, we read first, in verse 24: 'In wisdom hast thou made them all: the earth is full of thy riches', and then a few verses later, in verse 30, 'Thou sendest forth thy spirit and they are created'.

In the same way as it is possible to associate Wisdom with the creative work of the Holy Spirit, so we may perceive Wisdom in the Old Testament as fulfilling the Spirit's functions of guiding and inspiring. So we find such texts as: 'I therefore determined to take her to share my life, knowing she would be my counsellor in prosperity, my comfort in cares and sorrow.'[14] This is similar to the experience of those who feel they have been guided by the Holy Spirit, for it is as though wisdom far beyond their human understanding has been present in them, guiding their hearts and minds. To interpret this in terms of God's Wisdom entering the heart to guide human beings into deeper wisdom, is another way of describing an activity of the Holy Spirit with which many people are familiar.

This does not, of course, mean that the Holy Spirit *is* Wisdom. Neither the writers of the Old or New Testaments nor the later sculptors of Christian doctrine can claim to have got the Holy Spirit taped. Nor can we, however 'charismatic', say 'Here it is: this is a full description of the thing or person called the Holy Spirit'. Rather, we fumble our way towards expressing what we have come to understand of a certain aspect of God, and for that agonizingly difficult task we lay our hands on any stories that seem to elucidate the mystery, rifling the world's store of metaphors and poetic images in the process.

We have already discovered that one of the earliest ways in which the Jewish people conceived of the action of God in the world was in terms of breath or wind, *ruah*, and that this word was therefore used in their description of the Spirit of God. Similarly *Wisdom*, another way of understanding the action of God in relationship with people, appears as the breath of God: 'She is a breath of the power of God, pure emanation of the glory of the Almighty.'[15] Here the same word, *ruah*, is again used for the breath of God. This ties the concept in with the New Testament, where, at Pentecost, the Holy Spirit sweeps into the upper room to animate everyone there, 'like a rushing mighty wind'. If we accept Wisdom as another way of addressing the Holy Spirit, then we will find fruitful material in the Wisdom books which will help us to understand that, although the disciples of Jesus might have been taken over by the Holy Spirit in a rather new and unexpected way, there was nothing very new about the presence of the Holy Spirit in God's world. The following would be an appropriate prayer for any Christian in the period preceding Pentecost, as we pray for God's Spirit to come into our lives:

> With you is Wisdom, she who knows your works,
> she who was present when you made the world;
> she understands what is pleasing in your eyes
> and what agrees with your commandments.
> Despatch her from the holy heavens,
> send her forth from your throne of glory
> to help me and to toil with me
> and teach me what is pleasing to you,
> since she knows and understands everything.
> She will guide me prudently in my undertakings
> and protect me by her glory.[16]

Although St Paul does not hypostasize Wisdom, he does speak of wisdom as part of God and appears, in the first Epistle to the Corinthians, to associate it with the working of the Holy Spirit. He distinguishes true Wisdom from human wisdom, or philosophy, and claims that the Wisdom that he preaches, through the Spirit, is the Wisdom of God, which is beyond our understanding and which has been part of God since before time began:

> The hidden wisdom of God which we teach in our mysteries is the

wisdom that God predestined to be for our glory before the ages began. . . . These are the very things that God has revealed to us through the Spirit, for the Spirit reaches the depths of everything, even the depths of God.[17]

In post-biblical times Wisdom has been celebrated and revered more in the Eastern Church than in the Western Church, both in the dedication of churches and cathedrals and in the iconography of manuscripts, where the female personification of Wisdom, or Sophia, represents an aspect of the deity, often accompanied by Mary, through whom God was incarnate.[18]

Such a choice of patron for the major churches of Greece is perhaps unsurprising in a country which, in its pre-Christian ages, had traditionally honoured Athene, the daughter of Zeus and Metis. Athene was not only the goddess of war but also, in less bellicose aspect, she took after her mother in being the goddess of wisdom. In the same way as in Italy, where pre-Christian local deities easily became transformed into saints or local variations on the theme of Mary, such as 'the Virgin of the spring', in Greece it was perhaps a relatively uncomplicated matter to change allegiance from Athene to that Wisdom who was now ecclesiastically respectable, namely the Wisdom of God.

Although appearing, iconographically, as a woman, Wisdom is sometimes associated with the Word, or the second person of the Trinity rather than the third. Thus John Meyendorff identifies Wisdom with the Son: 'la Sagesse dont parlait Salomon est bien identique au Verbe né de la Vièrge'.[19] Bulgakov, too, in *The Wisdom of God*, more often associates Wisdom with the Son than with the Holy Spirit, though he does also recognize the validity of the alternative association: 'In the divine self-revelation, in the Ousia-Sophia, the "Spirit of Wisdom", the Holy Spirit, represents the principle of reality' (p. 78); and, 'we can say that the Holy Spirit too *is* Wisdom' (p. 75).

Several of the early Church Fathers identified Wisdom with the Holy Spirit, in particular Theophilus of Antioch in *Ad Autolicum* and, following on from him and most probably conversant with his work, St Irenaeus, the bishop of Lyon, in *A Discourse in Demonstration of the Apostolic Preaching* and in *Adversus haereses*.[20]

Irenaeus distinguishes between the Word, which was incarnate in Jesus, and Wisdom that is the Holy Spirit of God: 'rightly and fittingly is the Word called the Son, and the Spirit the Wisdom of God'.[21] This distinction is frequently reiterated in the *Adversus haereses*, particularly in the fourth section, where he uses the expression 'Wisdom which is Spirit'.[22] What he presents, in fact, is a sophisticated doctrine of the Trinity, in which both Word and Wisdom are in God from before all time:

Now that the Word, that is, the Son, was always with the Father, we have shown by many proofs. And that Wisdom, which is the Spirit, was with him before all creation, he says by Solomon, thus: 'God by wisdom founded the earth, and he prepared the heaven by understanding: by his knowledge the depths were broken up, and the clouds dropped down the dew'.[23]

From the latter part of the third century onwards, Wisdom was frequently identified with the second person of the Trinity and in time this became the standard way of integrating Wisdom into Christian theology. This alternative interpretation also has value in that it breaks down the sexual differentiation in God, by implying that although by an accident of birth Jesus was a man, he in fact represented the female principle of God.

But within common understanding of Wisdom there remained a strong link with the person of the Holy Spirit, as is evidenced, for example, by the number of Greek Orthodox churches dedicated to Saint Sophia which celebrate their patronal festivals at Pentecost, the feast that commemorates the coming of the Holy Spirit. It might be worth mentioning in this connection that Saint Sophia's day, which is on 30 September, is the festival not of the Holy Wisdom but of the legendary martyr, Sophia, who was said to be the mother of Faith, Hope and Charity. Again, to be allegorized as the mother of such gifts of the Spirit suggests a strong association between Sophia and the Holy Spirit.

SHEKINAH

There is the same adaptability between the second and third persons of the Trinity in another term, the Shekinah, which arose in late Hebrew.

In the earliest books of the Old Testament we find a particularly sharp awareness of the presence of God. People found that there were places and events in which they became conscious of God, almost as though they were face to face with the deity. But as God is spirit and cannot be seen, it was as if they looked on God through a veil, or as though God was hidden within a dark cloud.

So it is that in these early writings, as also much later in the vision of some of the Christian mystics, people coming consciously into the presence of God, whether in the Temple or in the kind of numinous environment that one encounters at the top of a mountain, identified the presence of God with a darkness or a cloud. When God gave the Ten Commandments to Israel, for instance, we read that everyone was made aware that something important was being imparted. But darkness prevented them from seeing God with their eyes:

All the people shook with fear at the peals of thunder and the
lightning flashes, the sound of the trumpet and the smoking
mountain;
. . . .So the people kept their distance while Moses approached
the dark cloud where God was.[24]

On other occasions God's presence was associated with refulgent light,
so that in Isaiah's vision of the Kingdom he promises that:

Your sun will set no more
nor your moon wane,
but Yahweh will be your everlasting light
and your days of mourning will be ended.[25]

Sometimes these two opposing images were drawn together so that the
presence of God was experienced as a cloud that covers but that is also
bright:

The cloud covered the mountain, and the glory of Yahweh settled
on the mountain of Sinai; for six days the cloud covered it and on
the seventh day Yahweh called to Moses from inside the cloud. To
the eyes of the sons of Israel the glory of Yahweh seemed like a
devouring fire on the mountain top.[26]

When Moses met God on the mountain and when Jesus was trans-
figured before his disciples as he prayed, the onlookers were aware first
of a cloud and then of brightness and light as these individuals came
into close proximity with God.[27] In relating the story of the
Transfiguration, Matthew, unlike either Mark or Luke, even uses the
term 'a bright cloud' to describe the overshadowing, so emphasizing
the relationship between this event and Moses' encounter with God on
the mountain.

Even today, people trying to recount spiritual experiences in which
they have felt particularly close to God tend to use similar language, full
of dramatic force and contradictions, as they speak of the mystery that
cannot be penetrated and the divine brightness that illuminates the
emotions and understanding. However much we believe that God is
eternally present with us, there are times and places in which we are
exceptionally aware of this presence, and in describing which we
struggle to express our experience of God.[28]

In the texts that refer to this presence of God there is generally a
reference to God's activity of 'dwelling', which is achieved by the use of
the Hebrew verb *shakan*, meaning to rest or to dwell. The early Jews
were faced with a very similar problem to our own in wanting to insist
on the otherness of God while at the same time recognizing God's
intimate presence in their lives. The trouble with attempting to
describe events in which people feel that they have come face to face

with God is that it is all too easy to slip into an anthropomorphism which diminishes our vision of God's transcendence.

It was partly to get round this problem that the later Jewish writers adapted the verb *to dwell*, which they found in so many of the stories where people felt near to God; they coined the word *shekinah* to denote this divine presence. The word was first used in its Aramaic form, *shekinta*, in the Targums, which were Aramaic translations of the Hebrew Scriptures; and then made frequent appearances in the Talmud, Midrash and other post-biblical Jewish writings. It does go some way towards expressing both the otherness of the transcendent and also the nearness of God:

> Every man would stand at the door of his tent and watch Moses until he reached the Tent; the pillar of cloud would come down and station itself at the entrance to the Tent, and Yahweh would speak with Moses. When they saw the pillar of cloud stationed at the entrance to the Tent, all the people would rise and bow low, each at the door of his tent. Yahweh would speak with Moses face to face, as a man speaks with his friend.[29]

The Jews recognized the intimacy of God's action and presence, at the same time as revering the divine transcendence and otherness; and it was the Shekinah that allowed this to be expressed.

In the original Hebrew of Exodus 25.8, God says: 'Let them make me a sanctuary that I may dwell among them.' Later, in the Targum, this becomes: 'I will cause my presence [Shekinti] to abide among them.' Similarly, in Exodus 34.6 the words 'And the Lord passed before him' become 'The Lord caused his presence [Shekinteh] to pass before him'. As G. F. Moore pointed out in 1922,[30] the Presence referred to in these texts is not something that takes the place of God, but a more reverent way of speaking of God which avoids some of the dangers of anthropomorphism.

The significance of this development for the present study is that the Shekinah is, again, a feminine word, and that the Shekinah, although not identical with what we mean by the Holy Spirit, does present similarities with that Spirit by describing the activity of God in relation to women and men.

On the face of it, the choice of the feminine gender to describe the presence of God has no more relevance than the use of *la présence* or *la personne* being used to refer to the presence or person of God in French.[31] However, the Jews who used this concept identified it as feminine more strongly than simply by linguistic convention, and in the rabbinical writings the Shekinah was hypostasized as a feminine being. From here it was but a short step to the Shekinah coming to represent the female element of God in Kabbalistic mysticism. But while the Kabbalists saw the Shekinah as an aspect of divinity, they also ascribed to her the relationship of daughter or wife of God, so tying her to a feminine principle that was dependent upon, and subordinate to, a masculine deity. In this way they lost that equality in God that is an essential part of our understanding of the Holy Spirit.

As with Wisdom, we cannot equate the Shekinah completely with the Holy Spirit. The mystery that we call by this name must, for example, include our subsequent knowledge of the activity of God in the New Testament and throughout history to our own day. Even limiting ourselves to a consideration of the Shekinah in Hebrew writings, there are differences, for one of the major contributions of the Holy Spirit in the Old Testament is as one who inspires or brings revelation, and these functions do not appear to have had any place in the Hebrew understanding of the Shekinah. But there are clear similarities between the two concepts, in that while we cannot see or know God, we can become aware of the presence and activity of God in our lives; we can experience the Holy Spirit of God. As the Israelites trembled before their vision of the glory of God and then through that experience came to understand what God was saying to them, so we, through the Holy Spirit, come first to an awareness of the presence of God and then in and through that experience find ourselves drawn into relationship with God.

As the Spirit hovered over the waters, the Shekinah hovers like a cloud or shimmering light. These compatible images, which suggest that at least to some extent the writers were trying to describe the same concept, give rise to a range of verbs that have long been associated with the Holy Spirit, such as 'overshadowing', 'indwelling' and 'hovering'. Although we may now wish to dissociate such activities from the nature of the feminine, it is worth recognizing that these activities are among those that have traditionally been designated as feminine; and so not only did both *ruah* and Shekinah bear a feminine grammatical form, but both were believed to be engaged in feminine activity in the world.

The fact that *ruah*, Wisdom and Shekinah are all feminine words has at least four interesting consequences. First, it takes away the ground from under the feet of those who insist on perceiving God as purely and exclusively male, when it is realized that many Jews and Christians through the ages have recognized these feminine concepts as essential aspects of God. Second, these feminine aspects of God have been represented in art as female figures, thus giving us icons of the deity in female form. Third, the use of such feminine terminology has given rise to thought forms that are feminine in character, as when we speak of Wisdom and all her children, which gives a picture of a closer bond of parenting than comes across when discussing the fatherhood of God; or the understanding which the Syriac Church gained into the mother-hood of the Holy Spirit, through the use of the feminine term for spirit. Finally, since all these terms are at least connected with our concept of the Holy Spirit of God, the wealth of material in which she appears in female form should reassure us that to use feminine terminology when referring to the Holy Spirit is neither as revolutionary nor as difficult as it might at first have appeared.

CHAPTER EIGHT

Who Is Our Holy Mother?

I beg you, oh, I beg you holy Virgin,
that I may have Jesus from that Spirit
through whom you bore Jesus.
Through that Spirit may my soul receive Jesus
through whom your flesh conceived the very same Jesus. . . .
In that Spirit may I love Jesus
whom you, from now on,
adore as Lord but gaze on as Son. [1]

FEMININITY AND SPIRITUALITY

Given the feminine gender of *ruah*, and more particularly the female personification of the presence and wisdom of God as the Shekinah and *hokmah* (Sophia) in Jewish thought, it should have been possible for Christian theology to develop a vision of God in which male and female were in balance. That such a theology did not emerge in the early Church might be said to be due in no small measure to the preaching and writing of St Paul, who, for all his new ideas, was inescapably a product of the chauvinist society into which he was born. While it is generally accepted that the institutional Church, following on from St Paul, has displayed a poor record as regards prejudice towards, and suppression of, women, it has not been so clearly recognized that this same institutional Church has also attempted to control the activity of the Holy Spirit.

There are good sociological reasons why a large organization, which sees itself as continuing throughout history, should exercise care and an historical perspective when faced with a changing world; but the fact remains that the Church has often shown itself to be a body that witnesses the winds of the breath of God and cries 'Enough and no more'. This occurred from the fourth century onwards with the rejection of texts that did not qualify for adoption as part of the recognized canon of Scripture; it happened for many people with the appearance of modern liturgies which were different from those in the *Book of Common Prayer*; it happens whenever a theologian or philosopher articulates a new insight or interpretation of the faith that does not accord exactly with previously accepted dogma; it happens in many a parish church when traditionalists quell requests for innovative liturgies, or refuse to allow anyone to remove the pews or change the music. All these cases betray a tendency to attempt to control the free activity of the Holy Spirit, to put God in a box away from real life.

But these are mere cosmetic details compared with the reaction of the larger and more traditional Churches to spiritual phenomena such as glossolalia and healing. The more spontaneous and free the activity, the more suspicion it arouses and yet, in the very earliest days of the Christian Church, these activities were understood as marks of the presence of God the Holy Spirit, special gifts that had been given to those who had let down the barriers between God and humanity: for some years it even looked as if these manifestations of faith would become the qualifying factors that proved that someone had indeed received the Holy Spirit.

This ambivalence, of course, also stems from the writings of St Paul, who, while forced to recognize the divine provenance of such gifts, was at pains to keep them under control as far as possible. These were activities that could not be rigorously controlled and that therefore have always been as much the preserve of the laity as of those ordained and brought under obedience to ecclesiastical hierarchy; and they were practised in the early Church, as much by women as by men.

Paul certainly did not forbid the practice of these gifts, but he did express reservations as to their value. The same ambivalence also surfaces in his attitude to women and may well have been related to it. Opinions vary as to the extent to which Paul was a misogynist, but this is not the place to pursue that discussion. Although he was severely criticized by women writers for some years, there is now a body of opinion that argues that the strictures Paul sometimes advocated against women were to help them fulfil their ministries within a society that would be excessively threatened by sexual equality. Others believe that Paul was more sinned against than sinning since the misogyny of his most notorious passages springs at least in part from the translations rather than the original texts.

Nevertheless, it would be difficult to absolve Paul from all charges of chauvinism, though that does not mean that he should be dismissed. Paul's writings, like anyone else's, are subject to the constraints of the society in which he lived. What is surprising as regards the position of women in the New Testament, is not so much that Paul accepted the assumptions of many of his peers on the intellectual, moral and spiritual superiority of men, but that Jesus displayed such an unconventionally liberal attitude in his dealings with women. Paul appears to have been a well-bred, highly educated religious man who was so cerebral and controlled that it took an experience of physical blindness to break down his resistance and allow him to see. But to complain about his suppression of the feminine is as anachronistic as it would be now to follow his guidelines slavishly for the conduct of women in church. There is also very little doubt that Paul often showed respect for women and worked with them as equals.

What is interesting in terms of our study of the Holy Spirit is not the extent to which Paul wished to suppress women, but the relationship between suppression of the feminine and suppression of the spiritual. Even if we ignore some of the more unpleasant strictures on women that have found their way into our Scriptures, it cannot be denied that Paul displayed a bias towards the male sex. It is also evident that he preferred masculine manifestations of the new life, such as preaching and teaching, to some of the less conventional and freer activities associated with life in the Spirit.

Whereas speaking in tongues was practised by both women and men, preaching and teaching were undertaken predominantly by men; and it is difficult to resist the conclusion that Paul would have preferred to keep it that way:

> As in all the churches of the saints, women are to remain quiet at meetings since they have no permission to speak; they must keep in the background as the Law itself lays down. If they have any questions to ask, they should ask their husbands at home: it does not seem right for a woman to raise her voice at meetings.[2]

> I am not giving permission for a woman to teach or to tell a man what to do. A woman ought not to speak, because Adam was formed first and Eve afterwards, and it was not Adam who was led astray but the woman who was led astray and fell into sin.[3]

Whatever his personal attitude to women might have been, by emphasizing the importance of public speaking on the one hand and attempting to ensure, on the other, that women did not practise this art, Paul effectively relegated women to the back seat in the Church, and guaranteed that they would be treated as second-class citizens within it. This is in sharp contrast to the treatment that God in Christ accorded to women, to whom was entrusted the teaching of the young Jesus, the comfort and friendship of his mature years, and the first revelations of his resurrection.

But the male-dominated activities favoured by Paul also represent the less spiritual activities of Christianity. Teaching and preaching may grow out of a spiritual life and may even inspire and guide others into adopting a spiritual life, but they are not, in themselves, particularly spiritual activities. This is first because they tend to be based in the head rather than relating to the whole person, and secondly, because they are addressed to other people rather than God.

Much of the fear of the female in the Church has been related to fear of sexuality, for the feminine has represented to men the two relationships in which he is potentially helpless and cannot dominate: that with his mother and that with a lover. Particularly in the case of celibates, women have threatened to weaken men's resolve and lead them into what they consider sin. It was easier to reject womankind as sinful, and to eschew the company of women as far as possible, than to live in equal loving relationship with them while at the same time exercising sufficient self- control to maintain their chastity. The fear itself is, of course, based on a chauvinist attitude towards women, for it contains the implicit assumption that women exist for the potential sexual enjoyment of the male sex.

The experience of falling in love is associated with the breaking down of the barriers of resistance and isolation and the changing of the *status quo*. Men who fear women sometimes do so simply because they fear the very love that threatens to take them out of themselves. The same could be said of the Holy Spirit of God, who frequently turns lives upside down, changing institutions, uniting the strangest groups into loving communities, and driving people out to live in solidarity with those who suffer and struggle. It is safer to keep such a Spirit at arm's length than to be swept up in the wind of God's love.

In the same way as the sexual drive is a powerful force that can be used for good or ill, one might also see spirituality as a powerful force for good which also contains potential for harm. Many young people in the twentieth century have suffered negative effects when their search for spirituality has led them into strange cults. Some people who have explored new ways of meditation have unleashed within themselves forces with which they cannot cope. Occasionally, charismatic groups have slipped over the line into mass hysteria, and gurus and spiritual guides have succumbed to the temptations of power and material reward. Iris Murdoch's novel *The Bell* warned us of some of the excesses that can be fermenting just beneath the surface in a community dedicated to Christian spirituality; and the experience of several of the religious communities of our own day, both traditional and innovative, would bear witness to the fact that far from representing a safe option in life, spirituality contains something awesome, powerful and possibly even dangerous.

This should come as no surprise to a Church whose birth was accompanied not by soft lights and gentle music, but by a rushing of the Spirit in fire and wind. The God whom we come to know through the Scriptures is God the Disturber, who takes hold of women and men in order to change their lives; who sends people off on what appear to be wild-goose chases, but in fact turn out to be strangely successful; who is Lord of the future as well as the past and who is never bound by creed, tradition or respectability. For God the Holy Spirit is not safe and predictable, she is alive and forever new. As she moves, winds rustle and flames flicker; for, as Hindus recognize, creation involves destruction as well as birth, and to be static is to be dead. It is not surprising that the Church should feel the need to control the activity of the Holy Spirit, for the Church is a human institution that cannot bear too much disruption; but we must at least be aware of what it is that is being done, and why.

In the first flush of enthusiasm for a radical new approach to life, those who witnessed the power of this Spirit at Pentecost were freed from the normal constraints of convention to such an extent that both women and spiritual activity became acceptable. Jesus had said that he had come to bring life in all its fullness: not because he was adding something to human beings which unfortunately got left out at creation; but because it is all there waiting to be released, so that it can bubble over into the whole of life. It is because God lives in people, in all their ordinariness and humanity, that allowing the Spirit to animate one's life must increase one's humanity, in the same way as becoming the mother of Jesus Christ increased the humanity of Mary. But that which is already within us is our reality, and to release and expose that brings us face to face with truth. This can be an uncomfortable experience until some of the dross with which we habitually protect ourselves has been purged away:

Go, go, go, said the bird: human kind
Cannot bear very much reality.[4]

When we meet our truth we find our freedom, for we discover that in the light of that truth there is no need for pretence, or reserve, or regret. It is this change of gear to a new way of living that releases in us the fruits of the Spirit, and that accounts for the intoxicating excitement of the first disciples at Pentecost: 'Where the Spirit of the Lord is, there is freedom.'[5]

But Pentecost and the ensuing life of freedom that was celebrated in the early Church also illustrate some of the dangers and disadvantages associated with freedom. Quite apart from the chaos that could result from too many people expressing their overpowering joy in strange languages, major assumptions and prejudices began to be challenged with uncomfortable frequency. Once Jewish laws began to be broken with impunity, once Gentiles began to be converted and enjoy the same privileges as the chosen race, and once women began to speak in church and exercise responsible ministries, where would this freedom end? Freedom brings risks and, since organized religion goes to some lengths to avoid risk, it was found necessary to impose control and direction on those people who believed they had been reborn into a new life that would soon be gathered into the life of heaven. Freedom was one thing for individuals who had been set alight by the love of God; it was quite another for an organized body of people who had to hand on the faith to succeeding generations.

The Church had exploded into life in a dramatic excess of spiritual activity, but, as it was trimmed into shape as an organized institution, echoing the hierarchical structures of the culture in which it was reared, its development was marked by the dominance of the cerebral over the spiritual. At the same time, what had been revealed as a message of hope for a more whole humanity gradually went through a process of masculinization. This masculinization was self-perpetuating, for as the feminine was excluded from Christianity, so fear of the feminine increased, making it difficult to reintroduce feminine elements into the faith.

This state could not long continue without appearing unbalanced and incomplete, and as anti-feminism became enshrined within the institution of the growing Church, so we find a cult of Mary being developed in order to compensate for the lack of femininity. Mary the mother of Christ would have occupied a crucial place in Christian history even if Jesus had been born as a woman, but once the Church began to develop into a male hierarchical institution that worshipped a male God, it became essential for some feminine element to be reintroduced to restore the balance that is part of the way the world is. But it would have been foolish to introduce the female in the form in which she was most feared, as a sexual being, and so a new woman was created, in much the same way as the old story said Eve was created, from the need and desire of man.

MARY

Little is known about Mary the mother of Jesus, though the hints as to her personality and behaviour that we find in the Gospels are far more moving and inspiring than most of the myths that developed later. It is little short of a tragedy that this young girl was purloined by the Church and recreated into a sexless, less threatening version of womankind, entirely unrepresentative of her sex, and the recipient of the fantasies and guilt feelings of men who seemed determined to forget that they had been redeemed.

There is nothing in the Gospels to suggest that Mary was exceptionally good. It is true that she is said to have found favour with God, but then so, for that matter, had humanity as a whole, which was about to receive God incarnate in human form. Mary is referred to in the Gospels as a virgin, which has presumably contributed to the honour accorded to her by men frightened of their own sexuality. But, quite apart from the fact that the word 'virgin' simply meant 'a young girl', there was nothing very unusual or pure about a young girl being a virgin in first-century Palestine: many still are even in the twentieth century. Over the years, Mary was mythologized by the Church to fulfil a need, to serve a specific function, and it is surely no coincidence that this safe idealized woman has been most revered by celibate clergy. To rob a woman of her sexuality in this way constitutes a form of rape, not respect.

If this all sounds iconoclastic, it is offered out of fervent love for Mary, whom I long to see honoured for what she was rather than what men wished she might be. Far from lacking due respect for the mother of our Lord, I have, throughout my adult years, practised a special devotion to Mary, particularly to the young woman portrayed in the story of the annunciation. But my love and respect have nothing to do with whether Mary had sexual intercourse with her husband: I sincerely hope she did. I am not interested in whether she ever sinned in any way, for within the new dispensation sin is forgiven and therefore does not separate us from God. I can see no point in speculating as to whether Mary died and decayed in the way we mortals do, with whether she received a special crown in heaven, or with whether she intercedes for human beings with God: such embellishments to history are the preserve of legend, not theology or prayer.

The Mary whom I venerate in my heart and try to celebrate in my living is the ordinary woman who was open to the unexpected and unconventional, and who put her own love and obedience to God above respectability. She is the one who listened more than she talked; who sang in joy and acceptance at the will of God as she saw it making waves within her own life; and who, watching her child grow, was prepared to observe and ponder in her heart rather than rushing in to manipulate or control when things did not go as she expected. Mary received no great honours or recognition, but was happy to stand aside as her Son matured into independent manhood. She suffered for him and did not run away; she was there at the moment of his disgrace and death as she had been at his birth. She then continued in community with other women, not setting herself aside as special, or even capitalizing on her more intense grief, but getting on with the business of living.

This is a woman who was aware of the overshadowing of the Holy Spirit, who dared to allow God to enter her womb and change the world from the inside; but who appears to have understood that rather than placing her at one remove from the rest of life, this increased her involvement with it. Mary was holy because, and in so far as, God the Holy Spirit was within her. But this sanctification by the Holy Spirit, which makes a person holy, does not change the natural order of things by making humans into gods. Within the divine economy, there is no need for such metamorphosis, for God can enter the human estate as it is. Mary should therefore be honoured for her humanity, not her divinity, for it was in her ordinary humanity that God was implanted. Whatever we understand about Mary's conception of Jesus, it did not take her out of normal life but embedded her more deeply within it.

The appropriation of Mary, therefore, to compensate the Church for a perceived lack of femininity betrays a regrettable lack of respect for the woman whom God chose to bear Jesus Christ. It was, in any case, based on the false premise that God, being male, lacks femininity. If, while creating a theology of the Holy Spirit the Church Fathers had retained the feminine form for speaking about God the Holy Spirit, this projection of divinity on to Mary might well have been unnecessary.

Mary and the Holy Spirit

In view of the fact that both Mary and the Holy Spirit represent for Christians feminine aspects of their faith, it is not very surprising that there exists a close connection between the two, both in the Gospel records and in the later devotions of the Church.

The most obvious connection in the Gospels occurs at the Annunciation when it is promised that the Holy Spirit will come upon Mary and overshadow her. With that divine conception within her she is filled, literally, with God the Holy Spirit and, as with the disciples later at Pentecost, her mouth is opened and her life changed. Because Mary was with Jesus in the key events of his life, such as his birth, his first miracle and his crucifixion, she continued to be aware of God's presence with her, and was thus filled with the Holy Spirit throughout her life. With her free and active co-operation with the Holy Spirit, not only in her initial *fiat* but in her later parenting and love, Mary also aligns herself with the freedom and activity of that Holy Spirit.

But as well as the contingent connections that can be drawn between Mary and the Holy Spirit in the Gospels, she and the Holy Spirit have been accorded a similar role by later Christians, as both being instruments of salvation. This connection was the subject of two papers that Cardinal Suenens gave to the Ecumenical Society of the Blessed Virgin Mary in 1981.[6] Recognizing that the choice of Mary or the Holy Spirit for this function relates to the distinction between Roman Catholicism and Protestantism, Suenens quotes Elie Gibson who had earlier written:

> It is possibly as difficult for Catholics to understand what Protestants believe about the Holy Spirit as it is for Protestants to understand what Catholics believe about Mary. . . . When I began the study of Catholic theology, wherever I expected to find an exposition of the doctrine of the Holy Spirit I found Mary. What Protestants universally attribute to the action of the Holy Spirit was attributed to Mary.[7]

It is interesting to note, in this connection, that at the end of the intercessions in the Anglican ASB Rite A, the prayers are summed up: 'Rejoicing in the fellowship of (N and of) all your saints.' While the flexible 'N' allows seasonal saints to be acknowledged, it is at other times common to honour the Holy Spirit at this point. In the Roman Catholic office, of course, this position is occupied by the Virgin Mary.

In support of the hypothesis that the Holy Spirit and Mary are employed by the different Churches to fulfil the same role, Suenens points out that, historically, Latin Mariology was most highly developed at the time when pneumatology was losing ground. For not only was Mary presented as a substitute for the femininity in God, which we mark particularly in the Holy Spirit, but she was also brought in to serve other functions that were properly the preserve of the Spirit. It is indisputable that Mary had a special knowledge of her son, Jesus. One can be very much less sure that she had either the clear awareness of the implications of her experience, or the theological sophistication that Suenens ascribes to her when he says:

> That divine presence which from her childhood she had been taught to venerate in one single spot on earth, there, whither only the High Priest might enter and then only once a year, upon the great Day of Atonement, she learns from the angel, she is now to adore within herself.[8]

According to Suenens, the purpose of both the Holy Spirit and Mary is to bring the faithful closer to Christ. But it is important not to be too seduced by the similarities between the way in which the Protestant Church has regarded the Holy Spirit and the way in which the Roman Catholic and Orthodox Churches have regarded Mary; for there remains a fundamental difference between the two, in that the Holy Spirit *is* God, while Mary is not. Mary may be holy, but she is not divine. If she were, then the birth of Jesus would accord with divine births in the mythologies of other religions and would have very little to do with incarnation.

The revelation of God in Jesus Christ, the Word and character of God which was built into the structure of the world much as our genetic characteristics are built into our DNA, is that God is present in humanity, not isolated from it. This was first shown in physical terms in Jesus and was then extrapolated in the dramatic outpouring of the Holy Spirit as people became fully aware, for the first time, of God within.

So while it is appropriate to love and respect Mary, we do not, after Pentecost, *need* her. Each time we rise from receiving communion we are in a similar situation to hers, of wonder at the physical presence of God within us. What we learn from the intensity of this experience is that the nature of God is to be with us always and to become part of what we are. If God is indivisible then we cannot speak of some people possessing more of the Holy Spirit than others. We may recognize and celebrate her more or less but, if God is within us, we, like Mary and like the disciples at Pentecost, are filled with the Holy Spirit. All that is at issue is how we cope with that amazing fact.

Mary and the Spirit in art

Because Wisdom is portrayed in the Bible as unambiguously female, images of her in Christian art have also been female. However, where this female aspect of God has caused embarrassment or difficulty, this has been resolved by extricating the concept of Wisdom from God and making her a person, or perhaps even a deity, in her own right. So, instead of being the wisdom of God, she sometimes appears more as a consort of God, separate and, necessarily, inferior to the Creator, even though the Old Testament writers speak of her as part of the creative process of God.

For those who have difficulty in countenancing portrayal of God in feminine form, it has also been tempting to assimilate Wisdom with the Virgin Mary. Bulgakov suggests that this is particularly prevalent in the Russian Church,[9] but it can also be witnessed further west. For example, while we have noted that several of the churches dedicated to Holy Wisdom celebrate their festivals at Pentecost, the major festival for the church in Constantinople was the Feast of the Assumption. But the majority of representations of the Holy Spirit occur in paintings and mosaics of the Trinity. Artists in general appear to have been daunted by the prospect of trying to portray that which is spiritual rather than material, although they have not always exhibited the same sensitivity over portraying the Creator, whom no eye has seen and who, being one and the same God as the Holy Spirit, is also Spirit.

Within the representations of the Trinity, the Holy Spirit herself is most often portrayed as a dove, which again is a feminine noun in Latin and Greek.[10] It is curious that the Spirit should be so frequently portrayed in this form, for there is no evidence at all that Christians have ever been under the misapprehension that the Holy Spirit *is* a dove. In the Gospel narratives we are told that the Holy Spirit descended on Jesus at his baptism 'like a dove'; but however 'like' it might have been, it was also clearly 'unlike' enough for no one to have been misled into imagining it actually was a bird.

It is certainly true that symbolism was widespread and sophisticated when literacy was rare. For example, the four evangelists are almost universally portrayed in their symbolic forms of lion, ox, eagle and winged man. However, whatever the intention behind the use of the bird to symbolize the Holy Spirit, one of its consequences was that it allowed Christian artists to avoid having to portray God in feminine form.

The fruits of the Spirit are all grammatically feminine, which is not very surprising since most abstract nouns in the classical languages are feminine. However, whether it is because of this linguistic gender or because these particular virtues have traditionally been interpreted as being feminine virtues, the fruits of the Spirit are generally personified in female form, as also are many other Christian virtues. So it is that in art, and more particularly in sculpture, we have numerous female images of the fruits of the Spirit as well as representations of the Wisdom of God in female form.

The other area in which, rather surprisingly, one can become aware of the femininity of the Holy Spirit is in the realm of ecclesiastical architecture. At the east end of many a cathedral is a small chapel known as the Lady Chapel, dedicated to Mary. These chapels, rather than housing the large and spectacular public services, are used for private prayer, for the ordinary day-by-day liturgy of the local community, for small and intimate gatherings which can replicate the 'upper room' experience. In such an environment one may become more aware of and open to the Holy Spirit, and come to perceive the Lady Chapel as an environment in which one celebrates the mother-hood of God the Holy Spirit, that 'lady', or feminine presence which we find in God and, if we are whole in our humanity and open to the divine spirit, within our own hearts as well.

The enclosed space of a Lady Chapel offers the safety of the womb, the regularity of worship echoes the beating of the heart, the nurturing stillness and quietness allow the inspiration of breath, or spirit, to animate the whole of life. The chapel becomes a generating plant of love, which, if directed solely towards Mary, might run the risk of becoming idolatrous, like the emotions aroused at the shrines of pagan deities. But if in such a chapel we feel ourselves held in the loving arms of God our mother, then we are rejoicing in the Holy Spirit, and will find that the 'Lady Chapel' takes on a quite new and exciting significance.

CHAPTER NINE

The Spirit of Freedom

Take mee to you, imprison mee, for I
Except you' enthrall mee, never shall be free,
Nor ever chast, except you ravish mee.[1]

THE MOTHER WHO LETS US GO

However much we might be nourished and sustained by our times of prayer and sacrament in a Lady Chapel, or its spiritual equivalent in our hearts, we have no desire to remain there. Instead we pray: 'send us out in the power of your Spirit', and as we leave we take with us all that we have received, to be used in our daily living. We are freed to live.

Here again the symbol of motherhood is a pertinent one, for the nature of true motherhood is to free, rather than to imprison, the child. Indeed, because child and mother are so completely one, it is only the mother who can effect this freedom. A child grows in the womb in order to be born as a separate person, and the period of gestation prepares the child for this entry into life. The mother then feeds her child; not simply because instinct guides them both to indulge such mutual enjoyment—ecstatic though that can be. The child is fed to sustain it when it is *not* at the breast. From then on, through weaning, training, educating and guiding, there follows a long process of enabling the child to embrace a full and mature life of freedom. It is the mother's wish that her child should learn to dress and feed himself or herself; to develop an independent mind; earn a living; and be capable of forming good relationships. However possessive a mother might be tempted to be, she will assist the child through this process of maturing until the child is free to operate as a fully independent person. Only if this process is allowed to take place can the child give himself back freely as a person to his mother; he is freed from the constraints of infancy in order to be himself. If human motherhood so yearns to make us free, how much more does God the Holy Spirit free us to be fully human.

A wrong concept of God's parenting can stunt our spiritual growth in the same way as bad human parenting can leave a legacy of emotional trauma. A faith that looks to God our Father to spoon-feed and cosset us is not going to help us grow into mature Christian adults. This is why Rosemary Radford Ruether rejects the parenting analogy for God:

'Patriachal theology uses the parent image for God to prolong spiritual infantilism as virtue and to make autonomy and assertion of free will a sin.'[2] Ruether extends this to the concept of mother as well, and she is surely right in rejecting such an image of a parent-God to whom we relate solely as an infant relates to a parent.

But Ruether's rejection of this image of God is flawed in two ways. First, it does not recognize the fact that the concept of parenting is no more static than the concept of God: it varies from country to country and has certainly evolved within our own culture over the last century. The father of today who changes nappies, helps teenagers with homework, and plays football with his offspring, bears little relationship to the Victorian 'pater'. Secondly, many people, particularly with the increase in life expectancy, have relationships with their parents for more years of adulthood than of childhood, and therefore the parenting/parented relationship between two independent adults is as potentially interesting as that between parent and infant. If we see a mother, for example, not just as one who brings us into life and nurtures us, but as one who yearns for us to be mature and free, who understands and loves us for what we are, who will stand by us as we muddle our own way through the world, then motherhood provides an illuminating image of God the Holy Spirit.

True freedom is born in the meeting between ourselves and God. By being, metaphorically, born of the Spirit, we become free to be that which we were created to be, children of God and temples of the living Lord. We are not, however, freed from mortality, from pain, temptation, or reality. God in us is part of the continuing pattern of incarnation, and to be in tune with the divine will we must be deeply embedded within the real world.

Because our union with God is based so firmly in the reality of our living in the world, it is there that we become aware of the Spirit at work, moving over the waters, bringing order out of chaos, working on the stuff of creation, active, astonishingly, in our own hearts. For the Holy Spirit *is* God's presence with us now.

Once one comes to trust in the Holy Spirit, the whole of life becomes sacred. I have already suggested that there is a sense in which the Holy Spirit completed the work of the incarnation, filling everything with God. So the Holy Spirit at work in the world of politics urges us to be politically aware and active; in society she drives us on to become agents of reconciliation, in human relationships she teaches us to care; and in our own hearts inspires us to offer love and thanks. But, above all, it is the Holy Spirit who brings liberty, thus freeing us to be children of God. We are not just freed *from* something, but freed *for* something.

Buddhists hope to be freed from everything in order, eventually, to attain Nirvana. Christians, on the other hand, recognize that when in this life we are freed from one thing, we are freed 'into' something else.

For the process of liberation is an entering into freedom, not into nothingness. If a prisoner escapes from prison he might find himself being less free if he has to live on the run. In the same way as peace is more than the absence of war, so is freedom much more than escape from prison or a rejection of constraints. It is a positive life-enhancing quality, not a negative flight from restrictions.

It is because we are free 'within' rather than 'without' reality that form and structure can assist freedom rather than limiting it. Great poets such as Shakespeare or John Donne, for instance, adopted what appears to be the strict discipline of the sonnet form in order to write poetry that is free. The constraint of fidelity in a good marriage, or of celibacy in the religious, can, rather than restricting the activity of loving, free a person to partake of much freer and fuller loving relationships with other people than would have been possible outside that commitment. Jesus, in his earthly ministry, freed people from sickness, guilt, neuroses and mistaken ideas about God. Those people became free to live more fully because the chains that bound them were broken. Then at Pentecost this freedom rained down on all who turned to the God who had been revealed in Jesus Christ. They discovered, and began to live out, their own freedom.

But Pentecost was not just one moment in time. In so far as it is part of divine time, it is outside the limits of human chronology and exists as an eternal mystery that can be experienced by the Christian as a continuing event. We do not just experience the coming of the Spirit once and for all, but constantly receive the overflowing of God's love in the coming of the Holy Spirit in our lives. We too become free to enter into life, rather than to opt out of it.

The excitement experienced by the disciples at Pentecost came from the sudden revelation that they were indeed free. Because God was within them, they were no longer subject to sin, to law, to the old system of rewards and punishments, nor to the separation from God that they had hitherto assumed was the normal condition of humanity: 'The reason, therefore, why those who are in Christ Jesus are not condemned, is that the law of the spirit of life in Christ Jesus has set you free from the law of sin and death.'[3] But how is this freedom manifest in our ordinary lives? St Paul writes in terms of our being freed *from* bondage *into* 'the glorious liberty of the children of God',[4] and this offers us a useful model for what it means for us to be free. When we have considered what it is that we are freed from, we will be able to explore that 'glorious liberty' and look at some of the practical ways in which we can exercise our freedom.

FREEDOM FROM...

The first, rather obvious, area of release is that we are freed 'from *sin*'.

Of this truth the New Testament record and the writings of the saints leave us in little doubt. But, rather surprisingly, many Christians appear to be reluctant to accept the implications of this liberation; and it is easier to find expressions of guilt over our sinful nature than of rejoicings over the collapse of the power of sin.

Sin is part of our human nature, part of the way the world is, and we are liable to run into severe difficulties if we do not give due credence to this fact. But Jesus, unlike many prophets before him and religious leaders since, did not make a song and dance about sin. Instead he offered the good news that we can be *freed* from sin. What we have learned about the nature of God and the world from the life and death of Jesus is that sin has no power; that whatever we have done we can be forgiven, and enter a new relationship with God and the world. The reason why sin in an unredeemed state is so serious is because it casts its long shadow forward to interfere with all our actions and relationships. It is this shadow that threatens our freedom.

We are free, not because we are no longer tempted, nor because we never succumb to temptation, but because if we face our sins honestly in the light of truth, open ourselves up to the infinite love of God and trust divine mercy, then we leave those sins in the past where they belong. Confession and absolution do not wipe away the natural consequences of sin: the murdered person will not come back to life however repentant the murderer is, nor will the murderer necessarily receive clemency from temporal courts of justice. But if the murderer is truly repentant and is prepared to have his life 'turned round' by the love of God, then he should accept that he has been forgiven and that guilt is to be put behind him. God loves him as he is now, not only as he was *before* he committed his crime.

The case of the murderer is, of course, an extreme example to illustrate how absolute God's pardon is. If we confess our sins and believe we are forgiven and absolved by God, then we must live out this belief in gratitude and hope. If we live in the glorious God-filled moment called the present, which is also eternity, shadows from the past cannot imprison us. We are, now and for ever, free to be. Some people prefer an intermediary to whom they can confess and who can then assure them of God's forgiveness; others learn to trust the loving relationship they have with God, and go through the process of confession and absolution at the Eucharist or in their own private prayer. Whichever method we choose, we must accept the implications of that absolution and rise knowing ourselves to be entirely forgiven, cleared in the eyes of our loving mother–father God.

One of the darkest shadows cast by sin is *fear*. If only we could be freed from our fears then individuals and nations could live in peace and trust, the wolf could lie down with the lamb, and the small child play on the adder's den.[5] When the disciples received the Holy Spirit at

Pentecost, fear fled in the face of this greater power, and the women and men who had huddled together in fear went out to speak and preach in public, to break the conventions of society and religion; even, in time, to face hardship, torture and death. The Holy Spirit had freed them from their fear.

If we were to analyse wars between nations or the breakdown of personal relationships, we would probably find fear to be the motivating force far more often than any of the other vices such as greed or lust: fear of another person's power over us, fear of our feelings for them, fear of making fools of ourselves, or fear of being let down. But when we have been filled with the Spirit of God, understood the nature of the incarnation, allowed ourselves to become part of God's loving in the world, then the energetic wind of God can whistle through these situations, cleansing and healing, freeing us from fear.

Once we begin to experience this freedom from sin and fear in our own lives, then we gain confidence to reject other forms of bondage and the shackles of this world fall to the ground. The early disciples, for instance, living out their Pentecost experience, 'all lived together and owned everything in common; they sold their goods and possessions and shared out the proceeds among themselves according to what each one needed'.[6] This desire to be free of *materialism* by becoming part of a sharing community has characterized the Christian life throughout its history, but has often appeared almost impossible to achieve. It is no wonder that St James calls the love of money the root of all evil, for time and time again the accumulation of wealth and prestige has stealthily wound around church institutions, binding those within and robbing them of their liberty. In every age, from the desert hermits, through to the medieval friars, the flower children of the 1960s, and to new experiments in community living today, individuals have rediscovered the potential for freedom that appears to flow from detachment from material goods.

St Francis, of course, exemplified this freedom, in his 'marriage to the Lady Poverty', and many since have longed for the simplicity and freedom of the life he chose. But poverty itself can also imprison; and having seen television pictures of those who wait for death in the dungeon of famine, or those within our own society who are caught in the traps of homelessness or unemployment, we should be aware of how insulting it is to be romantic about poverty.

The medieval Italian poet, Jacapone da Todi, understood that to be liberating, poverty must reside in the relationship a person has to possessions rather than in whether he has enough to live on:

Povertate e nulla havere
et nulla cosa poi volere
et omne cosa possedere

en spirito de libertate.[7]
[Poverty is naught to have and nothing to desire: but all things to possess in the spirit of liberty.]

Those who are prepared to live in the Spirit, thanking God for the present and trusting God for the future, can be signs to the world that a person's value resides neither in their possessions nor in the size of their pay packet; that the accumulation of wealth, far from leading to happiness, has a tendency to diminish—rather than increase— freedom. The same applies to those other baits of the world, status and power, which are dangled under our noses with their promises of freedom and happiness. Whatever advantages they offer, freedom is not one of them.

These chains only wind their way around our ankles because convention persuades us that they are important and we find it easier to conform to such well-worn conventions than to break loose. *Conformity* allows us to relax and feel comfortable, to act with some degree of self-confidence, and to know where we stand in relation to other people. But it also has heavy doors that slam shut to imprison the unwary, by convincing them that they must behave and speak and think in exactly the same way as others.

Conformity is a drug dispensed by many institutions that wish to control their members. Through its sleepy attractions, the Church has often gained control over its laity and persuaded them to toe the line. Non-conformity in itself is not a virtue, but if we live in the present with the God whose identity is I AM, then we must dare to be free from the constraints of what we, or others, have always done. This applies to large issues, such as how we define our faith and live Christian lives in society, and also to small matters, such as the words we use and actions we perform within our liturgies. As we claim our freedom, always sensitive to the needs and abilities of others, so our lives are enriched and the faith we have so gratefully inherited becomes our own: dynamic, adaptable, realistic; and therefore a true sign of God's Spirit in the world.

Exodus theology

Part of what it means, therefore, to accept the freedom of the Spirit, is that we can be free from sin and fear, from the debilitating effects of conformity and materialism. Liberation theology may have found concise expression only in the present century, but the truth that it embodies is as old as time. We were created by God to be free.

The major event in the history of the early Jews, which sharpened their identity and confirmed their belief that they were a special race, was the Exodus, in which they were released from slavery and went out into the unknown to live out their freedom. When the Spirit of God anointed the writer of Isaiah 62, one of the main tasks that was set was the freeing of those who were imprisoned: 'to proclaim liberty to captives, freedom to those in prison'.[8] Time and again throughout the Old Testament we find prophets and warriors struggling to release the people of Israel from the domination of foreign powers, from the chains of idolatry, or the more insidious binding effects of wrong living.

Then, when the prophecy of Isaiah was fulfilled and the history of the Old Testament came to its full fruition in the person of Jesus Christ, we find the same clarion call summoning us to leave our chains behind. For the essence of the ministry of Jesus was the proclamation that this liberty is available to everyone. Consequently, all those who were touched by him were released: from sickness and sadness, from the constraints of legalistic religion, from human relationships based on duty rather than love, from ancient fears, and from the lack of confidence engendered by being at the bottom of the social scale. The final, ultimate, liberty that Jesus Christ declared through his life, death and resurrection, was the liberty of knowing that death is not to be feared since life in the fullness of God is eternal.

The first disciples entered into this freedom through the coming of the Spirit of Christ as a force that could animate their whole beings, and that had certain repercussions: 'The reason, therefore, why those who are in Christ Jesus are not condemned, is that the law of the spirit of life in Christ Jesus has set you free from the law of sin and death.'[9] The Day of Pentecost was a celebration of the new dispensation of freedom, in which all those who received the Spirit were freed from the limitations of fear and doubt, freed from the restrictions of language, and freed from the insecurities of minimal education and inferior social position.

It is thus no wonder that the Church's birth was more redolent of a dam bursting its banks than of a committee being elected. It should have been unthinkable for Christians to give up the freedom bestowed at Pentecost, but one of the sad and shameful facets of our history is the way in which the Church has so often compromised Christ's message of freedom, substituting more and different forms of imprisonment in each generation. So church history records the sad process by which those who believed that Jesus Christ had come to set them free became subject, yet again, to the bondage of legalistic moral codes; to denominational divisions and club membership; to fossilized creeds and dogmas bolstered at times by the fear of heresy; to institutionalized forms of worship; to élitism; and the concentration of power and influence in the hands of the few.

So it was that the Church that was born free lost this freedom and continued to do so in every generation. Each revival of spiritual life and each reformation of the Church reawoke this urge towards liberation, but, depressingly, the institution sank back each time into the warm comfort of its own prison. Even the charismatic movement of our own

day has lost much of that fresh celebration of freedom that characterized its early days, and so common is this pattern that it appears to be
a natural consequence of institutionalization.

Yet this same Church still pays lip-service to the belief that Christ
came to burst the strait-jacket of legalistic religion and to offer life in all
its fullness; that the Holy Spirit of God blowing where she wills is the
spirit of freedom that cannot be contained and ruled; that any form of
Christianity that constricts humanity, that inhibits spontaneous praise
and joy, that divides people rather than releasing them to find deeper
peace and love, cannot be said to represent God on earth.

If the Holy Spirit really is the Spirit of God, then nothing that we can
do is going to quell that force. Fear, conformity, tradition and lack of
self-confidence have all played their part in restricting Christians and
yet, again and again, we find the Spirit of God bubbling up to disturb
our assumptions, to shake us out of our complacency, and to catapult us
on into new life. For neither rules nor institutions, neither the passage
of time nor the dry rot of lethargy, can limit the activity of the
irrepressible Spirit of God; and we can witness today, as much as at any
other time in history, the Spirit blowing through the Church. Despite
fear, indolence and the desire to maintain the cosiness of the *status quo*,
we are frequently disturbed by the Spirit whistling round the corners,
urging us to get on with ecumenism, to develop the ministry of the laity,
to value women, to give priority to the poor, to live out the good news of
Jesus Christ in the world, to gather all people to each other and so to
God.

FREEDOM TO . . .

In Scripture the appearance of the Holy Spirit is generally accompanied
by words of movement: wind, breath, living water, flying dove,
tongues of flame. In the Creed, the first quality that we ascribe to this
dynamic Spirit is that of being 'the Lord the giver of *life*'; for the Holy
Spirit is divine energy and this force, which creates all things, is
incarnate in us, inspiring and animating our lives. To receive the Spirit
of God is not to lie in a warm comforting bath, but to be driven out into
the cold with a task or responsibility:

> Here is my servant whom I uphold,
> my chosen one in whom my soul delights.
> I have endowed him with my spirit
> that he may bring true justice to the nations.[10]

The Holy Spirit has always been associated with religious revolution,
with those movements that have challenged human inertia and
complacency.

Even in the Old Testament, many years before the events of

Pentecost, the Spirit is seen as that which changes people and drives them on to dramatic actions: 'And the spirit of Yahweh seized on Saul when he heard these words, and his fury was stirred to fierce flame.'[11] The writer of the Book of Judges, entertaining what we would now consider a rather primitive understanding of the nature of God, believed that Samson's amazing feats were performed when he was filled with the Spirit of God, thus we read: 'As he reached the vineyards of Timnah he saw a young lion coming roaring towards him. The spirit of Yahweh seized on him, and though he had no weapon in his hand he tore the lion in pieces as a man tears a kid.'[12] And, 'Then the spirit of Yahweh seized on him. He went down to Ashkelon, killed thirty men there, then burning with rage returned to his father's house.'[13]

With the greater knowledge of the ways of God imparted through the incarnation, the actions to which women and men were said to be inspired by the Spirit changed, but the force of that infinite energy was undiminished. So, in the New Testament, when Stephen was 'filled with the Holy Spirit', it was in order that he could face his own martyrdom.[14]

The stories of the temptation in the wilderness, in which we first see the humanity of Jesus meeting and wrestling with his divinity, take place within the context of Jesus being filled with the Holy Spirit. Matthew and Mark, in fact, speak in terms of Jesus being driven out into the wilderness by the Holy Spirit. Many Christians who have experienced spiritual struggle and the loneliness of their own particular wilderness, have looked back in gratitude later to recognize that it was the same Holy Spirit who drove them out to meet their challenge without all the usual supports of friends, religion and everyday life.

The prophecy of Joel looks forward to the time when this energy will animate all people, so that things really start to happen:

After this
I will pour out my spirit on all mankind.
Your sons and daughters shall prophesy,
your old men shall dream dreams,
and your young men see visions.
Even on slaves, men and women,
will I pour out my spirit in those days.
I will display portents in heaven and on earth,
blood and fire and columns of smoke.[15]

It was, of course, this prophecy of prodigious outpouring that the early disciples saw fulfilled on the Day of Pentecost.

The Holy Spirit may be a comforter, may come in a still small voice or gentle breeze, but she is a spirit of energy and power, appositely symbolized by gale force wind and threatening fire. For freedom is not a cosy option; it brings risk and responsibility. As the Spirit of God frees us to enter more fully into life, we engage with all the danger and unpredictability of the real world. 'When Christ freed us, he meant us to remain free. Stand firm, therefore, and do not submit again to the yoke of slavery.'[16] The purpose of the Christian life is not to live in an aseptic vacuum. The point of being freed from the fundamental sin of fear or from the niggling evils of materialism, status and power, is not to lose our humanity but to embrace it more fully and perfectly.

The Holy Spirit, who frees us to live, also frees us to enter into communion with God; we shall explore what that means later. But if the Spirit in us is God in us, uniting our life to the divine, the more fully we live, the more we reflect the being and life of the God whose Spirit is in us.

The incarnation has taught us that the nature of God is love, and so by receiving the Spirit of God we enter into that life of God which is love. If it is true that the whole being and nature of God is love, then in so far as God is in us and we are in God, to live is the same as to love. Everyone knows that the distinguishing characteristic of a Christian is meant to be love, and yet it is no easier to live this out now than it was for the Jews in first-century Palestine. Only if we constantly receive the Spirit, live the Pentecost experience daily, can we incarnate this divine nature of God in our own world. 'You were called, as you know, to liberty; but be careful, or this liberty will provide an opening for self-indulgence. Serve one another, rather, in works of love, since the whole of the Law is summarised in a single command: "Love your neighbour as yourself".'[17] We can only be free if we live in harmony with the way God has created the world, which means that we are called to love. Because our beings long for this love, we set up substitutes that drain us of our energy and bind rather than free us; but true love, such as is described in Paul's great eulogy in 1 Corinthians 13, frees because by practising it we live in God.

St Augustine's exhortation 'Ama et fac quod vis' (Love and do as you like) has often been criticized for not including concepts such as justice. I remain convinced that this is included within the dictum, so long as it is interpreted correctly. If we love God, entirely and utterly, we will love people entirely and utterly; and if we love in that way, then we will desire only their best interests. This does not mean that we will not make mistakes in our loving as in everything else, nor does it ensure that our loving will not be rejected or misinterpreted, taken advantage of or mocked.

Loving is certainly no insurance policy against being hurt; on the contrary, it is a recipe for vulnerability. The reason we should love is not to ease our conscience, or to enliven our social life, or to set a good example to others, but so that we might enter into life in the image of God, for which we were created. Julian of Norwich, writing of her revelations of God, said, 'God did not say "You shall not be tempest-tossed, you shall not be work-weary, you shall not be discomforted".

But God said "You shall not be overcome".'[18] To love is to enter into the life of God's kingdom, to let loose the Spirit of God in the world now, in our relationships with each other and with the Creator. But if we imagine that love is the great panacea that is going to make life easier, we will be in for some rude shocks. Powerful it might be, easy it is not; and unless forgiveness is at the heart of our loving, as it is at the heart of God's loving, it will be impossible.

Forgiveness

The hinge between what we are freed from and what we are freed into is forgiveness. On the one hand, we are free from sin because we are forgiven completely and irrevocably by God. On the other, we are freed to enter into life in the Spirit, to live holy lives, but we can only begin to do this when we learn to forgive. In other words, we are freed *from* fear, *to* love, *through* forgiveness.

In the same way as knowing ourselves to be forgiven is fundamental to our being freed from sin, so our forgiving is fundamental to our life of liberty in the Holy Spirit. Forgiveness is the essence of freedom, and those who appear most imprisoned are those who cannot forgive themselves or who will not forgive others or God. However badly we have been wronged, our refusal to forgive will harm us more than it harms those we will not forgive, for it wraps us up in our anger and self-righteousness, cutting us off from the divine presence in the other person and turning all our thoughts and emotions to the past instead of the present.

Although loving and forgiving are liberating, most of us will, at some time in our lives, find it difficult to forgive and love someone who has deeply hurt us. In such situations, rather than accepting the prison sentence of resentment and hatred, it is appropriate to pray for the Holy Spirit. When we cannot do it ourselves, we can ask God to pour out the Spirit of love into our hearts, to be our loving and forgiving. We pray: 'Come Holy Ghost our souls inspire, and lighten with celestial fire.'[19] We then accept the consequences, as we allow the wealth of God's love and mercy in us to go out to the other person. As the warmth of God's activity within us melts our resentment at having been wronged, we relinquish our hold on the grievance and find our wounds being healed. The cycle of anger is broken and we become free.

Only if we are thus enabled to forgive, regardless of the response, can we enjoy the freedom of living in love. Although in loving we become utterly vulnerable, we also become part of a force that is stronger and freer than any force on earth. It was this force that Martin Luther King relied on, and that enabled his vision and love to continue to burn, even after he himself had been assassinated: 'We shall match your capacity to inflict suffering with our capacity to endure suffering. . . . Do to us what you will and we will still love you.'[20]

Fruits of the Spirit

Through the grace of God we can choose to forgive, in the same way as we can choose to be forgiven by God. Herein lies our freedom. But love is not a matter of choice in quite the same way, for love is a fruit of the Spirit, and as such develops in us rather than being adopted through choice. To refuse to forgive is to choose the kind of attitude and lifestyle in which love cannot grow, and a life without love imprisons one within oneself.

This is the opposite of what happens when we accept the Spirit of God into our hearts. Paul tells us that we can recognize God's Holy Spirit in people's lives by the 'fruits' we see: love, joy, peace, patience, kindness, goodness, trustfulness, gentleness and self-control.[21] These qualities illustrate the freedom of the Spirit, for they are not duties that we owe to God; there is no point in exhorting ourselves or other people to strive for them as virtues, or even to develop them as qualities that will help us to minister to the world. They are fruits of life in the Spirit; in other words, natural consequences of living in a certain way.

A tree cannot produce fruit by determination or greater effort. If it is planted in good soil, where it may benefit from light, warmth and rain, if it is tended, pruned and protected, then fruit will form. Similarly, gritting our teeth and concentrating on moral fibre will not bring the fruits of the Spirit to maturity in our lives. But if we live in a certain way, open to the Spirit of God, then these qualities will freely and naturally follow and begin to characterize the way we are. We may ask God for them, but we cannot manufacture them ourselves. The result of living in the Spirit is to receive these gifts.

In the operations of nature there are no rewards or punishments, only consequences, and this natural consequence theory applies also to the way in which God normally operates in the world. The Ten Commandments are not laws to satisfy a despotic tyrant, but guidelines to help people to live happy and fulfilled lives. As with the rules for sonnet form that were mentioned earlier, such rules form the structure within which one can find genuine freedom.

The rich young man who came to Jesus[22] had not found happiness in his observation of the Law, even though he had found the basic precepts fairly easy to obey. The Commandments made life work for many other people, but they did not challenge the rich young man enough, or demand from him the response that would have made his life meaningful. Jesus suggested to him another way in which he might find true happiness and engage in life, but the rich young man considered the price was too high and went away disappointed. Jesus did not say that the man 'ought' to get rid of all his possessions, but that if he wanted to be fulfilled, that was the way to achieve it. In other words, he was not recommending a course of action so much as stating a fact.

The same is true of the Beatitudes: they are *descriptive* rather than *prescriptive*. Jesus is not recommending that we should strive to develop all the character traits that he portrays in the Sermon on the Mount; he is saying that it just so happens that life is like that. This is worth saying because it is not obvious. It is, in fact, contrary to what the world maintains, which is why the Beatitudes still tend to take us somewhat by surprise. For they suggest that the people we should envy are those who are not protected by the false securities of life, but those who are thrown on the mercy and love of God and break through into another dimension of freedom.

The same tendency towards description rather than prescription can be found in many of the parables that Jesus told, for he was far more of a story-teller than a moral teacher. Most of his stories had as their punch line neither a moral precept nor divine command, but a shrewd observation, an illustration of what life in God is about. The risen Lord, too, appears to have employed this method when he accompanied the two disciples along the Emmaus road. Many leaders would have viewed this as a last golden opportunity to instruct the disciples and outline important tasks for the future. Jesus, on the contrary, building on what the disciples already knew and the kind of people they were, helped them to understand the nature of things. 'This is what it's all about', he explained gently. 'It's obvious when you see it, isn't it?'[23]

For the Bible is not a collection of moral precepts, but part of the story of the glory of God in relation to humanity. It presents us with a description of reality and unfolds a vision of the way the world is and of our place within that world in relation to the God who constantly creates and loves all that is. Only by engaging deeply with that loving reality of God, by committing ourselves hook, line and sinker to life, which is love, will we enter into our own freedom: life in the Spirit.

CHAPTER TEN

Filled with the Spirit

Know then thyself, presume not God to scan;
the proper study of mankind is man. [1]

GOD IN THE PRESENT MOMENT

We have seen that the hope and promise of the Old Testament is of freedom for the children of God, conceived, at that time, in narrow terms. In Jesus Christ we witness a truly free person, liberating those with whom he came into contact, although this was limited, in his earthly life, to a numerically insignificant group. At Pentecost, and in our continuing experience of Pentecost, that hope and promise, that gift of freedom, becomes available to all. 'The wind blows wherever it pleases; you hear its sound, but you cannot tell where it comes from or where it is going. That is how it is with all who are born of the Spirit.' [2] So the Holy Spirit blows where she wills, leading us into freedom; but what is the nature of the freedom that comes from living in the Spirit?

The essential motivating force behind this liberation is that God always meets us where we are. That is what the Holy Spirit is, God present in us. This is why, in previous chapters, I have stressed the unity of the Trinity, rejecting the concept of a separate Father-God sending an emissary to act on his behalf; for the action of the Holy Spirit in the world *is* the activity of God being in people. Furthermore, God is a God who surprises people by bursting in upon their lives in the present moment, rather than demanding all sorts of conditions and changes before entering their lives.

It is not very surprising, given the circumstances, to find the disciples, on the evening of the first Easter day, hiding behind locked doors 'for fear of the Jews'. What is rather more noteworthy is that into that situation, fraught with cowardice and suspicion, the risen Lord, God in Jesus Christ, enters with the words 'Peace be with you'. There was no question of urging the disciples to pull themselves together in order to be worthy of such a vision, or striking a bargain that they would behave differently in the future. Jesus knew perfectly well what sort of people his disciples were, what they had been through and how they had failed; he met them there in their fear and misery, in the same way as he met the two disciples on the Emmaus road in their disappointment and bewilderment.

At the annunciation, Mary was greeted with love and respect just as she was. She was not given a list of ways in which she might improve her life in order to become a fitting mother for God. One of the most encouraging aspects of the Bible is that all the way through, in myth and in history, in poetry and in revelation, we find God meeting ordinary people and working the divine power and love in them just where and as they are. The consequence of such encounter with God is generally a life changed in various ways, so that the disciples became braver, Mary became a mother, and the prostitutes and tax gatherers whom Jesus met were inspired to live differently. Such changes, though, were always *consequences* of the encounter with God, never conditions.

Only if we understand that God meets us where we are can we make any sense of the diversity of situations in which people encounter the Holy Spirit. Quakers meet the Holy Spirit in silence, Pentecostalists in singing and swaying, monks in the repetition of the offices, Wordsworth in nature. If God is one and indivisible, then it must be the same Spirit whom these different people are coming into contact with; it is the people who differ, not the Holy Spirit. So it is that women and men have met God the Spirit in art and music, in the experience of falling in love, through study or sport, by undertaking pilgrimages to the East, or sharing the lives of the suffering or poor. God meets them in those situations because that is where those people are; and God the Holy Spirit is infinitely adaptable, moving ahead of us, laughing, leading us on into life.

If one looks around the congregation at a cathedral Sung Eucharist one will, in general, see people who have a love of music and choose cathedral worship for that reason. Because they enjoy music in other parts of their lives, God meets them there through that medium; for through the beauty of the music they encounter the Holy Spirit, they grow closer to God. Their experience of God may be different from that found in a Methodist chapel or a Catholic charismatic church, because they are different from Methodists and Catholic charismatics; but the God whom they encounter is the same and each meeting with God, each experience of receiving the Holy Spirit, is equally precious and real. The cathedral congregation worships God in this particular way not because that is the right way, or because it is especially pleasing to God, nor, on the other hand, because they are musical snobs who care nothing for true spirituality, but because they enjoy that particular music, it is meaningful to them, and speaks to them of the transcendent.

This applies equally to other religious traditions: the church one chooses to attend depends very little on theology or doctrine, but quite a bit on upbringing and peer-group habits, and a great deal on personality. There is no one right way of worshipping because there is no one right way of being a human being. Given this, it is not surprising that feminists today are meeting God the Holy Spirit in feminism. That is where they are as people, that is what they value and understand; so that is where the Holy Spirit will hover, guiding them to become more perfectly what God intended them to be.

Some churchgoers are taken aback when others claim to meet God through exploring Buddhism, through a caring homosexual relationship, or through involvement in organizations such as Christian CND or Greenpeace. But in all these places the Spirit is there waiting for us, and we should try to overcome our surprise that the Holy Spirit can meet other people in such diverse places. Furthermore, the fact that many people in Britain today do not like the trappings of going to church certainly does not mean that God the Holy Spirit cannot meet them where they are—at the pub, swimming in the sea, or visiting aged relatives.

What is more important than the particular circumstances in which we first, or even repeatedly, encounter the Spirit is that we move, eventually, into closer relationship with God and are not held back by the vehicle through which God met us. This applies to Mozart's *Missa Brevis* in the cathedral as much as to the feminism of the new generation of woman scholars; it applies equally to the beautiful words that first shed light on the mystery of God for us and to the dynamic community that drew us towards a certain church. It is tempting, when we have been happy with someone, to go back to the same place or attempt to do the same thing instead of accepting that the relationship transcends past activities and may well blossom more beautifully if we go forward into the unknown together. Similarly with our loving encounters with God, we must be prepared to let go of the gifts we have received in the past and move on into life in the power of the Spirit.

Although the Spirit meets us where we are, she is never static. The story of the Epiphany illustrates this by describing how the Holy Spirit appeared as a star in order to guide the wise men from the East. In the form of a star the Holy Spirit could so fascinate this group of people that they were prepared to leave home, work and country to undertake a quest that had all the hallmarks of a wild-goose chase.[3] God again used that which spoke to people where they were. But when the wise men reached the stable, they moved on into worshipping God; the star that had been so sure a guide was forgotten.

God spoke to Moses from the depths of a bush that was ablaze without being consumed by fire.[4] Someone less familiar with the countryside than Moses might not have noticed anything exciting, but Moses had spent enough time in that terrain to know that what he saw was far from normal. He was also sufficiently awed by what he saw to connect it easily with the power of God; and so, even while approaching the bush, he was in a suitable frame of mind to receive instructions that were not attractive in themselves and would obviously prove exceedingly difficult to obey.

God the Holy Spirit spoke to Balaam through the mouth of the donkey he had ridden all his life, to Job in the whirlwind, and to Isaiah in a magnificent vision based on the splendour of the Temple. God used miraculous portents and vivid dreams to get through to people simply because those concerned lived in cultures where these portents and dreams mattered and were meaningful. It is futile to ask why God no longer comes to us in burning bushes and dramatic decipherable dreams; if these are not the currency we understand and value, they are unlikely to be our meeting points with the God who refers to himself not as 'Once upon a time' but 'I AM'.

Perhaps we move closer to our own experience when we read the resurrection appearances of Jesus. Like Mary in the garden, we have peered through our tears and tiredness to discover that Christ was nearer than we had imagined possible. Like Cleopas and his friend on the Emmaus Road, we have talked through our bafflement with friends and found God's presence with us as we shared our hearts and our hospitality. Like Peter, we have returned to our daily work only to find the risen Lord waiting there for us in the humdrum affairs of life, able to guide us if only we will allow it. In our moments of deepest pain and fear, we have found Christ standing with us saying 'Peace be with you!'

GIFTS OF THE SPIRIT

Paul stresses that there is a diversity of 'gifts' of the Spirit, because there is such a diversity of people. There is no reason to suppose that the bestowing of such gifts is arbitrary: it would be more realistic to assume that God uses the natural gifts and propensities of people. So when the public speaker is filled with the Spirit she finds herself preaching, and the caring person healing: 'Our gifts differ according to the grace given to us. If your gift is prophecy, then use it as your faith suggests; if administration, then use it for administration; if teaching, then use it for teaching.'[5]

This is not to suggest that life-changing miracles do not occur, for we have plenty of evidence, even from the earliest days of the Christian Church, that they do. At Pentecost, as a result of a dramatic outpouring of the Spirit, a motley group of fishermen, tax gatherers and other wanderers discovered that through the Spirit of God they had the power to stir the hearts of multitudes. There have been many other examples since of shy people suddenly finding their tongues loosened as they were driven to preach, almost against their wills; or of the gentlest, most respectable of conformists being taken aback by the unexpected gift of tongues showered upon them in public.

But such miracles are most probably the exceptions that prove the ırule. If we believe that we are created by God, then certain gifts have already been bestowed on us by that Creator. There is no reason to suppose that the same God, coming into our lives in the form of the Holy Spirit, should fail to realize the value of these God-given talents and haphazardly give us different ones. In other words, in most cases one effect of living in harmony with the Spirit of God will be the discovery that the Holy Spirit makes us more *us*, for the Holy Spirit does not, in general, work against the natural order, but within it.

When Samson tried to live by God's Spirit he received more of the incredible strength that had marked him out from birth. One might well feel that it would have been better if Samson had received a spirit of discretion or diplomacy, the power of reconciliation, or the gift of right judgement, but he did not. He received more of that strength which was part of his own identity, and through that rather surprising gift he was able, in the eyes of the writer of Judges, to further God's cause in the world.

This, surely, is one of the reasons why the spiritual life at its best brings freedom, for through living in the Spirit we discover that we are indeed free to be what we most essentially are. One of the joys of a good marriage or an intimate friendship is the discovery that after all the constraints of childhood, in which parents, families and educational establishments may have conspired to convince the child that there is 'much room for improvement', a spouse or a friend can accept and love us as we are, so allowing us, at last, to grow into ourselves, to be the real us.

If our freedom depends to some extent on our ability to be ourselves, it is a necessary concomitant of believing that God made us. This does not mean one should take a Platonic line by accepting that there is a perfect 'us' somewhere in the mind of God to which we can try to approximate: there is no evidence for this belief, and indeed it is difficult to imagine what kind of evidence could substantiate such a claim. But we do believe that God created and creates the world, and that we are part of that very creation that God looks upon and sees that it is good. Living in the Holy Spirit helps us to be what God made, namely ourselves.

It is important to maintain this belief that God created and creates the world, for the Church tried fairly consistently for several hundred years to persuade us that the material and social world is a bad place and that God lives in the Church. The growth of the monastic tradition in the Middle Ages had some stunning effects in terms of forwarding education in the Western world; and the success of these institutions in building communities of learning, healing, industry and wealth constitutes one of the most fascinating phenomena in our history. But their very success led to a view that salvation, holiness and right living were only possible within the confines of a religious community, and that outside in the real world all was unredeemed darkness and sin. This misconception tended to be self-perpetuating, since those who wanted to live a religious life were shunted off into the monasteries, together with all the resources that were available at the time, often leaving the rest of society impoverished.

Even with the secularization of a large proportion of the clergy, there have been efforts to preserve this myopic view. An elderly cleric once described a young boy by saying: 'He's such a good Christian, I'm sure he'll go into the Church' (i.e. become ordained). If anyone can read or hear that statement without being deeply shocked, it indicates how even today the old lie has been perpetuated. It cannot be stressed often enough that Christianity is about living, not about going to church; and God's Kingdom will come on earth not when everyone becomes a vicar, but when the Spirit, through the agency of those whom she has touched, sanctifies all the world, the whole of life.

If the Holy Spirit makes us more ourselves, then this will include developing both our feminine and masculine qualities. However, within Western civilization, with its centuries-long inheritance of male domination in society and Church, it is perhaps more apposite at present to perceive the Holy Spirit helping to redress the balance by allowing us to become more feminine.

The world, including the Church, is full of great monuments to the masculine aspects of our personalities; now, at last, even in the Church, one can detect stirrings that suggest that qualities traditionally perceived as feminine are also coming to be appreciated and used. So where discipline has been valued, constancy now also has a place; where instruction has been emphasized, there is now room also for listening and understanding; where punishment and the word have predominated, awareness is growing that people also need nurture and touch.

Self-knowledge

Most of us only learn to *be* ourselves as we come to *know* ourselves. The Holy Spirit is a spirit of truth,[6] and our growth in understanding and truth starts with our own nature. We are unlikely to understand other people, the world, or the nature of God if we have no awareness or understanding of that part of the world which is our own reality.

This self-knowledge entails neither the glorification of the intellect (which leads to gnosticism), nor the navel-gazing popularized by some of the passing fashions of 'pop-psychology'. Instead, it is an understanding and acceptance of our own human nature: emotional, physical, spiritual and intellectual. This includes a proper assessment of our own ability; honesty about our reactions to other people; acceptance of our failings; a willingness to face up to past mistakes; and an awareness of other people's attitudes to us. But, above all, it implies a sense of worth that comes from knowing oneself to be deeply loved.

Such self-knowledge is no easy matter for such complicated beings as we are, with our inherited instincts; negative as well as positive childhood experiences; the struggles of adolescence; and the multi-tudinous problems that beset us in adult life. An understanding of oneself cannot easily be gained by an act of will, or learned from a book; it blossoms from a life lived honestly and courageously.

One of the interesting facets of old age is the way in which so many ageing people, while still themselves, appear to become 'more so', as their personalities become more defined and distinguishable. It is quite easy to see this in terms of negative characteristics, so that we perceive the chatterboxes becoming garrulous, the mean becoming miserly, the anxious turning into fusspots, and the loners into hermits. This being the case, those who have spent their lives in self-deception, avoiding throwing the light of understanding on their hearts, are least likely in old age to exhibit the wisdom that comes of knowing themselves.

But the exaggeration of personality traits in the elderly works in positive ways as well, so that the generous become more self-giving, the sensitive become pillars of wisdom and strength to others, and the cheerful exude happiness. Perhaps this is why the archetypical saint often appears as an old woman or man, for the passing of years allows the positive personality traits to mature, turning the peaceful into the serene, the religious into the holy. Those who have been honest with themselves throughout their lives may still discover some surprising things about themselves as they ripen into old age, but they are unlikely to have too many rude shocks in store.

One might feel that the set patterns of behaviour and personality that we detect in the aged do not necessarily reflect their true nature, but can simply represent programmed responses to recurring circumstances. That old man would not have become so bad-tempered if he had succeeded more at work, or that old woman might have been kind and gracious if her husband had not fallen in love with a younger woman. But what we most deeply are includes the strange mixture of events that have occurred in our lives and our reactions to them. So for the old, part of being and knowing oneself is to be aware of the way in which one's personality is setting as one advances in age. Perhaps for the young, it is equally important not to fantasize about how one will turn into a better person when circumstances change and life becomes a little easier.

We often discover ourselves by relating to others, especially in the context of human love, both erotic and that involved in friendship. Spending a great deal of time with someone who loves us but is not fooled by us can lead to levels of honesty which bring insights into the self which would be much harder to attain alone. This is why married couples who do not learn to be honest with each other, because they fear the hurt, actually do each other the gravest of disservices by taking away one of the most natural routes to self-awareness that has been vouchsafed to humankind.

To be loved and affirmed by the person who sees us when we are tired and crotchety, when we are hurt, or angry, or boring or selfish—and with whom we have managed, albeit haltingly, to share our struggles of mixed motives and hidden insecurities—is to learn our own true worth. We are privileged indeed if, when our self-confidence has been shattered through a bad relationship, or our natural vivacity quenched through perversity, someone who knows us deeply can look us full in the face and tell us that we are loved just as we are. If we withdraw from people to lick our wounds in secret, we cut ourselves off from this source of love which helps us to see ourselves honestly as God sees us, in the light of love.

In a rather different way, conflict and pain can also sharpen our awareness, if we are prepared to be open to them rather than snapping shut like mussels. To discover how one reacts when one is badly treated, and to understand why one has caused aggressive behaviour in another person; to know that one is hated and yet to discover resources of love; to be deeply wronged and explore what true forgiveness actually means: these are exercises that demand that we face our true natures and grow in understanding.

The arts also play their part in the development of our understanding of ourselves, particularly, perhaps, literature. By becoming absorbed in the lives of characters, whose inner workings we are allowed to witness more than those of the people we meet in our daily lives, we sift through a variety of experiences; we try on different personality types to discover which ones fit and which do not.

This is probably most dramatic in adolescence when children are learning about the world and wondering what is acceptable and what is not. Many families with teenage daughters have to go through the stage of living with an elegant Jane Austen character in the house, but given how few adult Elizabeth Bennets there are walking around, presumably most find, in time, that it does not quite fit in the rough and tumble of twentieth century life.

As an adult, the experience of reading literature can be similar to the 'Aha' experience described in Chapter 1. We watch Hamlet or T. S. Eliot's Becket, and we recognize parts of ourselves being played out before our eyes; we read how a hero or heroine behaves in fictional circumstances and we know in our hearts that that is, or is not, the way in which we also would behave. We listen to the spiritual search or revelation of the poet and our heart cries out: 'Yes, that is how I feel it too, but I never knew how to put it into words'. By observing how events progress in a fictional situation we are able to test out hypotheses of behaviour and attitudes; we can flip through 'pattern books of personality' and see which ones might fit and which ones never will.

As we come to see ourselves more clearly in the light of God's love and wisdom, so we will dare to delight in and celebrate all that God has given us. There is no po-faced template that the Christian should seek to emulate. Not only do we all receive different gifts of the Spirit, but we all receive different personality types and ways of being holy. The rowdy teenager, the angry young man, the raucous tale-spinner and the shy academic are all equally good examplars of the richness of God-created humanity. Rather than trying to be *reformed* into the likeness of an archetypical 'Christian', they can all remain true to themselves as they are *transformed* into the likeness of God, in whom is infinite variety.

An understanding of the Holy Spirit as God within us, making us more fully what we are, can shed some light on the difficult passage in which Matthew relates Jesus' words on the 'sin against the Holy Spirit': 'Anyone who says a word against the Son of man will be forgiven; but no one who speaks against the Holy Spirit will be forgiven either in this world or in the next.'[7] In general, the theories that purport to explain this passage are not consistent with belief in a loving and forgiving God. A God who is prepared to die out of love for sinners is hardly going to turn churlish in the face of one particular sin and mete out eternal damnation to those who commit it, while freely forgiving all the others.

However, if the Holy Spirit is God in relationship with us, then to cut ourselves off from our own truth and reality is to cut ourselves off from God. To deny, rather than affirm, life, to despair of our human condition, to fail to recognize the love of God, the Holy Spirit, at work in our own lives, is to distance ourselves from God. By 'losing our souls' we lose God. It is not that God punishes us for this sin, but that the sin itself cuts us off from our own truth and reality, from all that our life is meant to be, so that failing utterly to accept the truth about ourselves we deny the incarnate God.

In other words, this passage, like so many others, is descriptive rather than prescriptive. It is not that there is one sin that is so wicked that God must punish it in a particularly strict and vicious way, but that within the freedom God has given us we can actually deny all that God is, even though this means blinding ourselves to who and what we are. To deny the loving action of God in our own hearts and lives is to block that very vital energy through which we live. It is to quench the Holy Spirit.

As we saw earlier, Paul is quite clear that the different gifts that are given to Christians arise out of what they are. Whether one is inspired to stand up and proclaim the gospel in public, or live a quiet life of love and faith, or offer one's intellect for the instruction of others, depends on the sort of person one is. The Holy Spirit knows how each person may best be used for the glory of God:

> There are all sorts of service to be done, but always the same Lord; working in all sorts of different ways in different people, it is the same God who is working in all of them. The particular way in which the Spirit is given to each person is for a good purpose.[8]

It is the same Spirit who enables the linguist to communicate in many languages,[9] who steels the faint-hearted with courage,[10] who showers creative inspiration on the poet, artist or dancer.[11] For as people are infinitely various, so will they be given a variety of gifts with which to glorify God and bring others to live to the full the life that God has given them.

Healing

Given the life of Jesus and the apostles, it would appear that one of the gifts that the early Church most expected to witness was the gift of healing. To be healed is to become whole, which is to be fully oneself, even if some disease or disability is still part of what one is.

Throughout the ages people with the gift or knowledge of healing have worked through various channels to heal the sick, and there is no doubt that our natural abilities and our growing knowledge of medicine have been used to work God's healing power in the world. God has used the gifts that people possessed as a framework for the gift of healing. But apart from this rather mundane interpretation of healing, we are also witnessing today the growth of spiritual healing, which does not always appear to depend on medical science or even on recognized alternative medicines.

It is worth noting that when St Paul wrote to the Corinthians about the various spiritual gifts, he distinguished between normal healing and miracles: 'another again the gift of healing, through this one Spirit; one the power of miracles';[12] The miraculous healing practised by the early disciples and by a growing number of Christians today, could well be interpreted as a means of discovering one's true self. As, in response to the working of the Holy Spirit, we strip away some of the non-essential bits of our personalities, we lose those aspects that militate against our proper functioning as human beings. Those who practise a Christian healing ministry frequently stress that healing can take place in a person even when the known disease is not affected. This is consistent with my suggestion that healing is about discovering and accepting our true selves and that, incidentally, such discovery and acceptance will often, though not always, bring about a more healthy body. This would certainly accord with the modern understanding, which has taken so long to reach human consciousness, that we are whole psychosomatic creatures and that a great deal of our illness has an emotional or spiritual root.

To come, through the grace of God and perhaps through the prayers of others, to a state of awareness, in which we accept ourselves honestly and know ourselves to be loved, is certainly to be healed at a very fundamental level. If it enables people to come to this sort of health (or salvation), then it is hardly surprising that the practice and appreciation of the ministry of healing is growing.

As the ministry of healing is just one of the gifts of the Spirit available to the Christian, so being healed is just one of the manifestations of grace that come to us through life in the Spirit. As, through the Holy Spirit of God, we are freed to be ourselves, to fulfil our God-given potential, so the fruits of health, wholeness and salvation will have the chance to ripen in our lives.

Prayer

If God is the ultimate reality in life, then prayer, through which we explore our relationship with God, will lead us deeper into reality. St John refers to the Spirit who is God in action in the hearts of ordinary people, as the Spirit of truth. But this Spirit is also a personal God, and prayer is a loving encounter with one who sees all and knows us more than we know ourselves. In opening ourselves to the Spirit of truth we begin to uncover who we really are and co-operate with God in becoming the people whom God made.

Truth is essential to prayer and, in the same way as refusing to be open to other people tends to snarl up our relationships, failure to be open towards God will certainly get in the way of prayer. In prayer we interact with God, the ultimate reality of our lives, and that experience should lead us to a deeper knowledge of ourselves.

Prayer can clarify our vision so that we see reality 'more so'. This is particularly true of contemplation, which will be discussed in Chapter 11; but other forms of prayer, too, take us deeper into reality and truth. Intercessory prayer, for example, relies on our taking our stand before an omniscient God in order to share our innermost feelings about the world, ourselves and the glimpses of divine glory that we see in daily life. Confession confronts the reality of our own sin and failure, and praise delights in God's glory revealed in the world.

Self-discovery is not, however, a valid reason for undertaking prayer. One of the difficulties in discussing prayer is that Christians discover a number of benefits when they pray, and sometimes others perceive these benefits and want to receive them too. But when the benefits are desired as ends in themselves, they crumble into dust. I have been involved for many years in teaching religious dance and, naturally, those who practise this form of prayer find that they improve their physical fitness; but the whole concept of religious dance disintegrates if people turn to it as a means of keeping fit. Many people who have joined groups to learn contemplative prayer have had their lives changed as they discovered new power within themselves, but anyone who came to such a group in order to learn a technique that would release this power, would destroy the whole purpose and meaning of that group. The situation is reminiscent of the occasion in the Book of Acts when Simon the magician witnessed the power of the Holy Spirit in the apostles and thought that it would be useful for his conjuring tricks.[13]

The confrontation with reality that we call prayer is fertile soil for peace and joy; for as we see ourselves honestly and know ourselves to be loved by God, we discover that we are actually free to be ourselves and can work in harmony with God in us and in the world. We experience what it means for the Spirit to make us free:

Now this Lord is the Spirit, and where the Spirit of the Lord is, there is freedom. And we, with our unveiled faces reflecting like mirrors the brightness of the Lord, all grow brighter as we are turned into the image that we reflect; this is the work of the Lord who is Spirit.[14]

CHAPTER ELEVEN

Enfolded in Love

A condition of complete simplicity
(Costing not less than everything)
And all shall be well and
All manner of thing shall be well
When the tongues of flame are in-folded
Into the crowned knot of fire
And the fire and the rose are one. [1]

In these chapters I have attempted to draw together various aspects of our faith that relate to God the Holy Spirit. For reasons outlined earlier, this has been done within a framework of understanding in which the Holy Spirit is comprehended and addressed in feminine terms. To follow, in this way, the logic that is clearly implied by both theology and ancient practice, will allow, at least for some people, a much fresher and more accessible revelation of God the Holy Spirit in our lives today.

This appreciation of the femininity of the Holy Spirit has led, however, not to a statement on the status of women, but to discussion of the nature of God and the life of faith. What we believe about God will determine the way in which we relate to God and that, in turn, will be one of the major influences on what we are as people. It is possible to construct a religious system in which the predominant belief is in God as an all-seeing judge—and, as Victorian moralists discovered, this belief can be made to have far-reaching effects on the ordinary lives of believers. Conversely, the moment at which a Christian really discovers for herself that she is loved by God, will be the turning point in her life: it will allow her to love and be loved in all her other relationships. Calling the Holy Spirit 'she' affects our relationship with that Spirit in subtle ways, as we saw was the case with the early Syrian Christians who responded to the motherhood of the Spirit and so understood baptism in the Spirit as a new birth. [2] It can take us deeper into the heart of God.

WE BELIEVE IN GOD

There are three main principles that underlie everything in this book: first, that *God IS*; second, that *God is Spirit*; and third, that *God is love*. These are beliefs that are biblically based, but that are also confirmed through the ordinary experiences of life. They are beliefs that issue in action and make us the kind of people that we are.

God IS

First we define God and, in line with the self-denotation given by God to Moses, the theistic believer asserts that God IS. A God who *is* must be a present reality, not a past event. Not only does God exist, but God is instrumental and inherent in all that is. In creating the world, however millions of years that has taken so far, God said, 'Let there be . . .' and it was. God then considered it, looked on this reality that now was, and saw that it was good.

What we sometimes fail to understand is that it was essential that creation was good, for the God who is, is present in it. It was only with the advent of Jesus Christ that people eventually began to grasp that this is the nature of God and reality, that God both IS and is incarnate. Because of this we, as part of God's creation, are free to be, to enter into the I AM of God and celebrate the reality that God creates and sees that it is good.

Jesus Christ, in whom we see the meaning and mystery of God, did not come to proliferate religious practices but to bring in God's Kingdom. He preached that this Kingdom is not something distant and unattainable, but that it is present now, under our very noses if we will but look. 'Repent, for the kingdom of heaven is close at hand'.[3] John the Baptist had proclaimed this message, using it, in true Old Testament style, as a stick to beat his hearers into penitence. Jesus, although he also urged people to enter into new life, offered the gift of grace now, rather than the threat of retribution. He preached 'the Good News of the Kingdom' because, as in the best jokes and cleverest riddles, it is obvious once you have seen it: Immanuel, God the Holy Spirit is with us; all life is holy, for 'the world is charged with the grandeur of God'.[4]

This means that life in the Kingdom of God cannot be parcelled off and left to an after-life, but is concerned with the here and now. A religious life is one that engages deeply with all of life, and celebrates the world that God creates and loves. If we imagine that we must spend as much time as we can in 'church' activities in order to be holy, then we have completely missed the point.

God is Spirit

The second fundamental belief is that God is *Spirit*; and that therefore that which we find operating as the Spirit of God in the Bible, throughout history and in our own lives, that which we call 'the Holy Spirit', is God. Because this Spirit is present, and active, in us, we can relate to God as person to person. So, far from being an amorphous spiritual morass, the Holy Spirit is essentially personal. Being God, this Holy Spirit is available to everyone, not just to a Christian élite. She cannot be circumscribed by religious affiliation or legalistic definitions, but is energy, ubiquity, freedom and love.

Life is spiritual because our whole being responds to the being of God; spirit touches Spirit. We are not dualistic machines, part physical, part spiritual, but whole human beings; and our spiritual life is part of our ordinary life. There is nothing that the Spirit of God cannot sanctify, 'What God has made clean, you have no right to call profane.'[5] Peter was made aware of this by a dream, which came from the depths of his own understanding. As, through his release from the constraints of pigeon-holing life he became free to relate in love to Gentiles as well as Jews, thousands more women and men were freed to enter more fully into life, by coming to know God through Jesus Christ and the Spirit of God at work in their own lives.

God is love

Our third fundamental belief is that the nature and being of God is *love*. This belief defines God, but it also defines us since we are part of that creation which is the object of God's love. We therefore believe that God created and loves us for what we are, that we have value and that human life is worth living.

Our freedom grows out of our certainty that we are loved and can therefore celebrate being completely ourselves. Through our life in the Spirit we inherit the complete life of love that God offers us and through living fully in the Spirit of God we become free, with all the risk and fulfilment that this implies. Freedom should therefore be a characteristic of the Christian, as it was of Jesus.

This freedom permeates the whole of life, from the insignificant to the ultimate. We are free in small ways, such as in the language we use in worship and whether we sit or stand or kneel; for we worship the infinite God, not the form of service used in any church. We are free to explore different denominations and world faiths; to learn from the wisdom of the Holy Spirit in those traditions more of the greatness of God, and to pursue our own spiritual path with integrity.

But our freedom extends to the whole of life in the world, not just to church activities. Because God's Spirit is with us we are free to enter into relationships, trusting that God values all people everywhere, that the Holy Spirit dances in the meeting of eyes.[6] We are free to love, for love is behind, within and beneath the whole created order and we were made to enter into loving relationship with all. We are free to risk pain and turmoil because, although we are capable of suffering at least as much as anyone else, we have seen the suffering of all divinity and all humanity in Jesus, and have learnt through experience that through the cross comes resurrection. We are free to get life in perspective, treasuring it, celebrating it, holding it as a gift from God; free not to worry about tomorrow, even though tomorrow may look unpromising, for nothing can fall outside the love of God. We are free to live, because human life was the vessel into which God's self-giving love was poured, and we are free to die because death is not the end of life.

SACRAMENTS OF LIFE

If the Holy Spirit broods over our ordinary life, sanctifying all that is, then one might be led to ask what the value of specific prayer and worship might be. If one is deeply engaged in life, what place is there for prayer and sacraments? Religious activity can provide an escape from reality, and the Church has offered sanctuary to many who could not face life in the 'big bad world'. An institution that offers an opiate to dull the edge of living may be cosy, but can never represent the Word of God on earth. All religious activity, to be valid, must grow out of normal experience and feed life in the real world.

A sacrament is 'an outward and visible sign of an inward and spiritual grace given unto us'.[7] Being concerned with definitions and rules, the Anglican rubrics name but two sacraments that were 'ordained of Christ our Lord in the Gospel', namely, baptism and Holy Communion. In addition, the Church recognizes five others: confirmation, penance, orders, matrimony and extreme unction.[8] There it draws the line, as though such a list could possibly exhaust the myriad ways in which God the Holy Spirit draws aside the veil and allows us to see, to know and to love the beauty and wonder of God.

The Eucharist is for many Christians the most powerful of all sacraments because of the real connections and reverberations it creates at every level of the participant's consciousness. In this sacrament the whole of life becomes transparent, so that in it and through it we see and rejoice in the eternal God, transcendent and immanent. We orient ourselves entirely towards God; shed all that separates us from God; greet those around us as part of the Body of Christ on earth; gather all our concerns and the prayers of the whole Church into the loving embrace of our Father/Mother; and take our place as part of the communion of saints that transcends time and space.

As we concentrate our attention on the bread and wine, we begin to celebrate the blessedness inherent in the ordinary. We discover that this Holy Communion, which brings us face to face with the God who *is*, who is Spirit and who is love, is a way *into* life, which is love, which is God's. Regular Communion can therefore set up a rhythm in which all life is drawn into the spiritual and the sacrament is taken with us into the world: 'Send us out in the power of your Spirit, to live and work to your praise and glory.' But this sacrament is given by God, not by the Church, as is acknowledged in the provision that the validity of the sacrament is independent of the worthiness of the minister. One may receive Communion from someone who is living in the darkness of hell and still experience the flood of divine grace; for the sacrament is dependent on the recipient, not the one who administers it. There are plenty of people, clerical and lay, who have gone through the motions of Holy Communion for one reason or another without letting it impinge on their life, and for them the words and actions by themselves do not manifest a sacrament. To cling on to hatred or anxiety, to refuse to forgive another person, to fail to care sufficiently for those mentioned in the intercessions, to reject life rather than celebrating it, is to choose to take part in a ritual rather than a sacrament.

Equally, matrimony does not become sacramental just because the Church gives its blessing at the wedding. Thousands of couples who have married in church with all the trappings of religion never receive through their union the inward and spiritual grace that allows them to become complete people, filled with the Spirit of God. It is not the wedding that is the sacrament, that leads us into the mystery of God's love, but the marriage; and strictly, the Church does not marry anyone, but stands witness while 'those whom God has joined together' marry each other and begin to explore through their love and commitment something of the nature of God. In and through each other they move deeper into God.

When marriage is a sacrament, it is so because of two people's experience of married love: the erotic celebration of another person; the trust and loyalty that is built up over years of living together through thick and thin; the breaking of the boundaries between one person and two, so that sharing is natural and the happiness of the other is the touchstone for one's own delight. It is a sacrament because the agony and the ecstasy, the self-sacrifice and self-fulfilment, make real to the woman and man involved the love of God for each of us, and the response that we all have it in us to make.

This is why, far from limiting ourselves to seven sacraments, we can constantly discover the infinite sacramental quality of life. No one has written about the sacrament of parenthood, and yet in observing and receiving the unconditional love of small children, watching their absorption in the present moment, their total commitment to life, their inexhaustible capacity for forgiveness, for wonder, for generosity and for fun, many parents begin to understand, to trust and to respond to the life-giving love of God.

It is surely no coincidence that the sacraments that are recognized by the Church relate to those moments of our lives when we become most deeply engaged with life: our life commitment to another person or to a vocation; grave illness or the death of someone close to us; the birth of a child; or our coming to terms with the sin we have committed. It is at these times, when we live life in the raw, that the incarnate God can break through our defences and bathe our lives in grace. But, as de Caussade suggests,[9] to abandon onself to the love of God is to take part in a constant sacrament: the sacrament of the present moment.

The value of the recognized sacraments is that they can form in us a habit of seeing the glory of God breaking through the ordinariness of life, so that more and more of life becomes sacramental. So we become aware of the sacrament of friendship, celebrated, perhaps, when two friends turn towards one another in a crowded room, and in the meeting of their eyes convey to each other the totality of their shared interests and humour, their trust and enjoyment of one another. Other common sacraments might include the sacrament of shared pain, the sacrament of natural beauty, the sacrament of hilarious comedy and the sacrament of gardening.

If these sound too mundane to be classed as sacraments, then that is just the point about them. Through such ordinary actions the grace of God floods our beings, in the same way as God comes to us in the earthy sharing of the bread: our staple food. The ordinary is both transformed and unchanged; we see through the accretions of habit to the searing significance of its reality, and we ourselves are changed through our experience of it. For example, the act of gathering spinach in a small town garden, or tomatoes from a window box, can be such an act of joy and gratitude that one's whole body and heart become a song of praise, a living grace.

These actions are not, of course, always sacramental, and can be performed with no awareness of God whatsoever. But then neither, as we have seen, is the Eucharist or matrimony always and necessarily sacramental. For an action, an order of words, a relationship, becomes sacramental at the point where a response is elicited from us. Grace is freely given, but it is not received until we accept it. Sexual intercourse is one of the most perfect expressions of our love for another person, and yet the existence of prostitution indicates that this same activity can be performed where love is absent. Similarly, the Eucharist will be, for many Christians, their most intense experience of meeting with God, but that is a result of their own attitude and response, rather than their adherence to a particular liturgy.

This openness to the sacramental quality of all of life leads, in itself, to contemplative prayer, for to take part in the sacrament of the present moment is to enter into contemplation.

CONTEMPLATION

We have seen that the word used by the Hebrews for the Spirit of God was *ruah*, meaning breath or wind, and how in seeking to describe the activity of the Holy Spirit, various writers used metaphors of breath (in the case of Elijah) and wind (at Pentecost). Chapter 7 began with some words by the poet Gerard Manley Hopkins, in which he refers to the Virgin Mary as 'world-mothering air', a title that is even more appropriate for the Holy Spirit who surrounds and embraces us: 'This air, which, by life's law, My lung must draw and draw.'[10] Considering the frequent association of Mary and the Holy Spirit described in Chapter 8, it should come as no surprise that such a designation should be interchangeable.

Since our relationship with God, the one in whom 'we live and move and have our being', is intimately connected with our living, it may be significant that contemplative prayer, in which a person's whole attention is focused on God, should, in some traditions, have been understood in terms of an awareness and control of the action of breathing, through which we live.

The religion that has contributed much to this method of praying is Hinduism, in which 'pranayama', or control of breathing, constitutes a major part of the yogic discipline through which adherents concentrate mind and body entirely on God, in order to attain *samadhi*. With the enrichment of Christianity, which has come about through living in more multicultural societies, many Christians, too, have begun to learn that pranayama helps them to become still and receptive to God the Holy Spirit.

There are at least three ways in which pranayama can contribute to prayer. The first of these is in its function of relaxing the body while increasing, rather than diminishing, awareness. Prayer *can* be undertaken anywhere at any time, but there are physical and mental states that are more conducive to prayerful activity than others, in the same way as there are physical and mental states that are more conducive to sleep, to study, or to happiness. A tense body, an overactive or anxious mind, a fragmented awareness, make prayer so difficult for most Christians that it is worth exploring ways in which such obstacles can be removed.

Anyone who has held their breath to aid concentration in the face of a difficult task, or concentrated on breathing deeply to allay butterflies in the stomach before a public engagement, or stretched and taken a deep breath before settling down to sleep, has some understanding of the way in which our breath can be used to assist in a task or attain a required state of mind. Similarly in prayer, correct exercise of breath control can help us to come more immediately into a physical and mental state in which we can be open to the love of God.

Secondly, breath can also be used in the activity of praying itself. Following the established wisdom of Eastern cultures, as well as some of the saints within our own Christian tradition, many Christians have found it helpful in prayer to adopt a mantra. This is a single word, or a short phrase, which is repeated over and over again, so that it gradually sinks down from the conscious mind into the heart of the one who prays. Generations of Orthodox Christians have engaged in this activity as they have repeated the 'Jesus Prayer': 'Lord Jesus Christ, Son of the Living God, have mercy on me, a sinner.' The more this prayer is repeated, the more it becomes indistinguishable from the one who is praying.[11]

In Roman Catholicism the telling of the rosary is an equivalent mantric activity, in which the words are so familiar that one comes to an awareness of them that is far deeper than any cerebral understanding. One might even say that the Lord's Prayer, which unites all Christians and which is probably recited more than any other prayer in the world, constitutes an extended mantra, although its length precludes it being held whole in the mind and heart of the worshipper.

In general, a mantra should be very short and should not require any progression of thought from one part to another. The purpose of it is to allow the word to pray in us, rather than for us to pray the words. In this way, rather than struggling, with our finite minds, to comprehend the infinity of God, we can become still while our spirits commune with the Holy Spirit of God. In adopting this form of prayer, one can either take different mantras, according to one's present needs or the pattern of the liturgical year, or one can adopt a permanent mantra that is one's own and, by regular repetition, becomes part of what one is. Common Christian mantras are: God is love, thank you God, Maranatha, Come Holy Spirit, Jesus is Lord, Holy, Kyrie eleison, Alleluia.

The discipline of concentrating own's whole being on the mantra stills the mind and infuses the whole body with the essence of those words, which lead us deeper into the heart of God. Mantras can be used without pranayama, but when the mantra is 'breathed' and the normal activity of respiration provides the rhythm for that particular form of prayer, the effect of this discipline of prayer is enhanced. Further, since the activity of breathing comes to be so closely identified with the recitation of the mantra, it becomes second nature to slip into repetition of the mantra at other times, so that gradually more and more of one's life 'becomes' the mantra.

This is also true of the third way in which pranayama can assist the process of prayer. As well as reciting the mantra in one's heart in time with the rhythm of breathing, one can pray through the activity of breathing itself. Words have their place in prayer, as does silence; so do both dance and stillness. In the process of bringing the focus of our lives on to God, there are many differing activities that can become part of our prayerful offering to God. But one of the most appropriate is the act of breathing itself. If, in our quiet times of prayer, we learn to draw in God's love with each in-drawn breath and to share that love with all in need as we exhale, if the regular rhythm of our breathing embraces the beauty and goodness of creation and reflects our acceptance and affirmation of the gift of life, if the meeting of air and flesh to issue in life sharpens our awareness of our oneness with God, then our breathing will be a vital part of our praying.

The implication of adopting this form of prayer is that if we can learn to pray through our breathing, then, gradually, even if we cannot devote more of our day to the recognized activity of praying, it becomes possible to pray for more and more of the time, while walking, working, even sleeping. As our breathing becomes our prayer, we can continue to pray while undertaking all kinds of other activities in the world, so breaking down the distinction between prayer and living. In the limit, pranayama would enable us to be in a state of constant prayer and adoration of God. In other words, through the ordinary physical activity of breathing, we incline our hearts more and more towards God and engage in that form of devotion that has traditionally been called 'prayer of the heart'.

This is to be 'in prayer' rather than to be 'saying our prayers', and some people describe it in slightly different terms as the experience of the Holy Spirit praying in us. In view of the interpretation of Spirit as air, it is surely no coincidence that as we draw in air and allow prayer to become the rhythm of our normal living, so we find ourselves at one with the Spirit of God, who prays in us. Many poets have the impression that they do not compose their poetry in any real sense, but that a good poem 'writes itself' by emerging from the depths of what the person is. Similarly, many Christians have the experience that, at its best, a life of prayer is one in which prayer arises from deep within a person; that rather than our praying *to* God, God in fact prays *in us*.

The child in the womb has as much need as anyone of a supply of oxygen to the blood. But only by being part of the rhythm of the mother's breathing can the child receive that oxygen through the placenta. This offers us yet another analogy based on the motherhood of the Holy Spirit, for, as the Holy Spirit prays in us, we are held and given life in God. For the Christian, living in the Holy Spirit is natural, just like breathing. Prayer is not just an optional extra, but our life blood, our entry into life as it is meant to be, the air we need to breathe if we are going to live fully.

Several of the spiritual writers have described contemplation in terms of entering into truth and reality, becoming part of the 'Isness' or 'I AM' of God. One of the reasons, too, why art has so often assumed a connection with contemplation is that part of the function of art is to present the truth of what is being represented, not a copy of it.[12] Martin Heidegger, referring to van Gogh's painting of a pair of peasant's shoes, concludes: 'Van Gogh's painting is the disclosure of what the equipment, the pair of peasant shoes, *is* in truth. This entity emerges into the unconcealedness of its being. The Greeks called the unconcealedness of beings *aletheia*.'[13]

When we appreciate a work of art aesthetically we perceive something of the truth that the artist is trying to share with us, and we offer an unconditional response. Similarly, when we fall in love, we see more in the beloved than any idle onlooker would perceive and we respond to the truth of the person as we recognize it. Our spiritual life bears some relationship both to an aesthetic response and to a falling in love. But prayer embraces more totally the whole of life, since all of life is part of the creation of the divine artist and we fall in love with God in every manifestation of love we encounter in the world.

So, through prayer, we come to breathe in harmony with the way the world is and our breathing both elucidates this metaphorically and assists the process physically. This kind of prayer is an integral part of life, not a peripheral activity, and everything matters enough to be part of our experience of prayer. Prayer, therefore, while taking us deeper into relationship with God, also leads us more fully into life, since through it we come to a richer appreciation of the incarnate God who is deeply embedded in our life; the Holy Spirit of God, breathing in us, praying in us, living in our living. In view of this, it is no wonder that the adoption of the practice of contemplation can have far-reaching effects in the lives of individuals as they allow the love and power of God the Holy Spirit to live through them in the world. As they trim their sails to the wind of the Spirit, their whole life begins to move in the right direction.

There is nothing exclusive about receiving the Holy Spirit; it is open to all of us, for part of what it means to be human, made in the image of God, is that we have access to that Spirit: 'and one Spirit was given to us all to drink'.[14] The true test of charismatic experience is not how 'good' it makes us feel, but whether it takes us more deeply into life, or simply marginalizes. As we breathe in harmony with God's Holy Spirit, so we find the fruits of the Spirit maturing in our lives and the world is changed from the inside out. To live in the Spirit is not to be on a constant spiritual 'high', but to become more and more transparent to God in the ordinariness of our daily lives.

SPIRIT OF LIFE AND LOVE

When Jesus told his followers to 'be perfect',[15] he used the word that the Greeks translated *teleios*. The implications of this word have more to do with being complete, than with exemplifying morally good behaviour. In other words, Jesus was urging us to be fully ourselves, to let our completeness as human beings mirror the completeness of the God who created us and all that is.

If the world is created by and for love, then our completeness will obviously reflect this principle of love. So it is not surprising to find that the New Jerusalem Bible translates Christ's command as: 'You must therefore set no bounds to your love, just as your heavenly father sets no bounds to his'. For in this divine game, love is both giver and gift. When we love, we long to give, whether it be the little gifts we offer as tokens of our love, or the generous giving of our time, our trust, ourselves; for giving is the natural outcome of loving. For God, too, loving leads naturally to giving: 'God so loved the world that he gave'.[16]

If we are to accept the conclusions of the fourth-century theologians who worked out the doctrine of the Trinity, when God 'gave' Jesus Christ, it was God who was given. Small wonder, then, that in Jesus we see the pattern of love in action. Similarly, when the Holy Spirit was 'given' at Pentecost it was, again, God who gave God, and in this Spirit we ourselves bear within us the being of God and thus enter into love. As the Spirit of God was given to us, so we received the greatest gift of all. For the Holy Spirit is God, and God is love. As far as St Augustine was concerned, if we do not love we do not have the Spirit—it is as simple as that: 'Ask your inward parts: if they are full of charity, you have the Spirit of God.'[17]

St Paul sets Christian love above any of the spiritual gifts that help us to spread the gospel of Christ in the world. This is because God is love and so, by entering into love, we enter into God. If we enter the love of God, we engage in the world that God has created and we learn to live fully in love. This life of love is both ordinary and amazing, human and divine. It is as ordinary and homely as our indrawn breath; and it is as divine and wonderful as the gift of life that is ours for as long as we breathe. Yves Congar describes this Spirit of Love as both concrete and sublime:

> I would say on reflection that the charity that the Holy Spirit places in our hearts is not only sublime, but also very concrete. . . . The principle of that charity is the Holy Spirit of God. The most ordinary and concrete aspect of it forms an integral part of the most sublime element.[18]

The life of love is ordinary because it is concerned with our living our imperfect, muddled lives in the world as it is, facing our own peculiar pains and shortcomings. It accepts the given of the world, and gets on with the business of living in relationship with that world and the variety of people with whom we come into contact. It is ordinary because it is the activity of people who share a common humanity with all who starve or suffer, all who fight for life or shun it in despair.

But the life of love is also divine, because it is more than we could possibly achieve in our own strength. It is divine because it is not dependent upon 'deserving'; nor is it reserved for our friends and families, but goes out freely to those who hate and fear us, those who have wronged us, those we do not understand; to the warped and the wicked, the starving and the satieted, the handicapped and the hopeless. It is the pattern that we have learned to recognize in the whole of creation and that we see exemplified in the life and death of Jesus, the Child of God. Through engaging in it ourselves we, too, become one with God the Holy Spirit.

The confluence of the very ordinary with the very divine is what we normally call incarnation, for it defines God, I AM. This God, the most Holy Spirit who is Creator and Redeemer of the world, became a human being to show that we too are part of this divine love, that that is what life is about and what it is meant to be. In other words, God made us and gave us ourselves, or our freedom, so that we might freely give ourselves to each other and to God.

For it was in love that the Holy Spirit brought the world to birth; nurtured humanity to a vision of God; overshadowed Mary at the annunciation; manifested herself in Jesus Christ; and filled the Church with new life. That new life of love is offered to us all as children of God. Only if we dare to live in this love can the fruits of the Spirit ripen in our lives. For as this love springs up and bubbles out of us, we grow to be at peace with ourselves and with the world. We enter into the beauty of creation, offering joy and thanks for life, celebrating all that is, living out our love for people, but also for colours, sounds and scents, for whatever physical activity we are capable of, for life and all that is. We receive abundant life.

This gift of love is the one absolutely essential quality that defines a Christian; one who, by the power of the Holy Spirit, has entered into God's loving in the world. It is not something one does, but something one is; and through this divine love all of life becomes sacred, as we live in God, the most holy and life-giving Spirit.

Notes

1 We Believe in the Holy Spirit

1. Edwin Muir, 'The Annunciation'.
2. Yves Congar (1983, vol. 1, p. 12) suggests an interesting parallel between ancient and modern interpretations of oil as a symbol of the Spirit:
    What sport and athletics did in the ancient world, cars and machines do in the modern world: they enable us to appreciate the play of this substance that penetrates everywhere, spoils nothing and, on the contrary, facilitates the smooth functioning of each part.
3. See Chapter 4, n. 9.
4. John 3.8.
5. For example, Congar, Barclay, Lampe, Taylor, etc.
6. Alfred Tennyson, 'The Higher Pantheism'.
7. Rom. 8.26.
8. One of the earliest versions of the text of the Lord's Prayer actually has the words 'May the Holy Spirit come' rather than 'Thy kingdom come'.
9. Eph. 6.18.
10. Acts 17.25.
11. *De Trinitate*, book 1, ch. 3.

2 Language, Church and God

1. W. R. Yeats, 'Maid Quiet,' in Yeats (1933).
2. Wittgenstein (1958), 569, 570 ff.
3. 'The Relation of Habitual Thought and Behaviour to Language', in Whorf (1956).
4. *Briefing*, vol. 17 no. 9, p. 160.
5. Hence the General Synod Liturgical Commision's report, *Making Women Visible*, January 1989.
6. In this book, exclusive theological language is avoided as far as possible and the discipline has been adopted of avoiding personal pronouns that refer to God. Very occasionally, such avoidance would have led to language that was unacceptably contrived, and no apology is made for using masculine terms in such instances. We do not write within a vacuum, and it is desirable to work with an awareness of the history and tradition that forms the context for our thought.
7. Charles Davis and John McDade explored the question of whether the maleness of Jesus Christ was contingent, and what that implied, in the *Tablet*, 18 and 25 February 1989.
8. See Morley and Ward (1986).
9. Sarah Coakley, in 'Femininity and the Holy Spirit', in Furlong (1988), argues that the ascription of femininity to the third person of the Trinity contributes to the subordination of the female.

10. See Chapter 5.

3 The Eternal Triangle

1. e. e. cummings, 'one's not half two', Penguin Poets 1963.
2. 1 Pet. 1.1.
3. For example, 1 Cor. 6.11; 1 Cor. 12.4–6.
4. Matt. 28.20.
5. 2 Cor. 13.13.
6. For example, 1 Cor. 3.23; 11.3 and 15.27. See also John 14.28.
7. Deut. 6.4.
8. 'God as Trinity: An Approach Through Prayer', in Doctrine Commission of the Church of England (1987).
9. John 15.26.
10. Though later declared a heresy and squashed as firmly as possible, Arianism was sufficiently widespread and respectable in its day to have stood a chance of becoming orthodoxy. Arius was a fourth-century Alexandrian presbyter, who found that his knowledge of and devotion to both God and Jesus Christ would not allow him to accept them as identical. While he venerated Jesus Christ, he refused to believe that a man who was born, suffered, wept, got angry, sweated and died could be the transcendent God who was, Arius believed, beyond all suffering.
11. The icon was painted c.1410–1420. It was originally for a monastery at Zagorsk, but is now in Tretyakov Gallery, Moscow.
12. Gen. 18.
13. Matt. 3.
14. Acts 2.
15. Matt. 17.

4 God Is Spirit

1. e. e. cummings, 'if i have made, my lady'.
2. 'We do well, therefore, to remember that the word "Spirit" itself is a metaphor, just as the words "Father" and "Son" are also metaphors.' See Taylor (1972), p. 7.
3. Ezek. 37.1–14.
4. Ezek. 37.6.
5. John 19.30.
6. 1 Cor. 2.11.
7. The term 'dualism' refers to the belief that mind and body are separate entities. Within European philosophy, the problems of dualism stem from the writings of the seventeenth-century French philosopher, René Descartes, who attempted to outline the interaction between these two different entities. Twentieth-century philosophy and the development of psychology and medicine have led people to question the possibility of isolating mind and body as separate components. In some ways, the desire to drive wedges between mind and body might be seen as parallel to the artificial distinctions between the 'persons' of God.
8. Gen. 1.2.
9. The translators of the 1985 New Jerusalem Bible challenge the interpreta-

tion of *ruah* in this context as 'Spirit' and speak instead of 'a divine wind sweeping over the waters'. The short note that accompanies the text dismisses, in a rather cavalier fashion, the many translations that have associated this wind with the Spirit. Even if, as is difficult to assess, the original writer of this verse had in mind a primaeval porridge with wind blowing over it, the meanings and associations that have accrued to it have related it to the Spirit of God. For what the verse attempts to describe, in picture language, is that before all else, God was; and if God was, the Spirit moved.

10. Ps. 51.11.
11. Job 33.4.
12. Hag. 2.4–5.
13. Judith 16.14.
14. John 4.21–24.
15. Gal. 4.6.
16. Cyril of Alexandria, *Commentary on John*, IX.
17. Rom. 8.11.
18. Phil. 1.19.
19. Gal. 2.20.
20. Luke 12.12.
21. Luke 21.15.
22. John 20.17.
23. *Les Chants de Taizé, les Presses de Taizé, 71250 Cluny, France.*

5 What Is Femininity?

1. 'The labelling of these capacities as masculine and femine simply perpetuates gender role stereotypes and imports gender complementarity into each person's identity in a confusing way. . . . We need to affirm not the confusing concept of androgyny but rather that all humans possess a full and equivalent human nature and personhood, *as male and female* [Ruether's italics]'. See Ruether (1983), p. 111.
2. The concept of androgyny as applied to God is not new, but was used by the Shakers in the nineteenth century.
3. For example, see Vetterling-Braggin (1977), pt 2.
4. Carolyn Korsmeyer, in 'The Hidden Joke: Generic Uses of Masculine Terminology', explores some of the connotations of such different uses of masculine and feminine terms. See Vetterling-Braggin (1977), pt 3.

6 The Feminine Face of God

1. From 'Ash Wednesday', by T. S. Eliot. See Eliot (1963).
2. Hayter (1987).
3. Exod. 34.6.
4. Isa. 41.13.
5. Isa. 54.10.
6. Isa. 66.13.
7. G. W. H. Lampe, 'Women and the Ministry of Priesthood', *Explorations in Theology*, vol. 8, London, 1981, p. 97.
8. John 1.1.
9. Julian of Norwich (1966), 59.

10. Ps. 104.30.
11. Acts 17.28.
12. Ps. 17.8.
13. Eph. 3.17.
14. 'God's Grandeur', in Hopkins (1960).
15. 'But the parent model for the divine has negative resonance as well. It suggests a kind of permanent parent–child relationship to God. God becomes a neurotic parent who does not want us to grow up. See Ruether (1983), p. 69.
16. Gen. 1.27.
17. Congar (1983), vol. 3, p. 155.

7 World-Mothering Air

1. Gerard Manley Hopkins, 'The Blessed Virgin compared to the air we breathe', in Hopkins (1960).
2. Strictly, in the singular it is feminine only in grammatical use, since the 'ah' ending is a phonetic ending rather than defining the feminine form. However, in the plural, *ruhoth*, it is feminine in both form and usage.
3. Deut. 13.11.
4. There are one or two occasions when *ruah* takes on a masculine form, e.g. Isa. 32.15, but it is generally believed that these represent solecisms rather than intentional changes in the use of language.
5. E. Hennecke and W. Schneelmelcher, *New Testament Apocrypha* (London, SCM, 1963), p. 164.
6. Aphrahat, Demonstration 18, verse 18.
7. John 3:3–6.
8. From an anonymous Syrian Orthodox service, quoted in Brock (1979), p. 65.
9. Brock (1979) p. 4.
10. Para. 17.
11. Prov. 8.23.
12. Prov. 7.27.
13. Wisd. 7.7–12.
14. Wisd. 8.9.
15. Wisd. 7.25.
16. Wisd. 9.9–11.
17. 1 Cor. 2.7 and 10.
18. See also Chapter 8, section entitled 'Mary and the Spirit in Art' on p. 86.
19. 'L'iconographie de la sagesse divine dans la tradition byzantine', in Meyendorff (1974), p. 276.
20. *Adversus haereses*, written about A.D. 180, set out to refute the errors of Gnosticism and the heretical doctrines of Marcion, and in so doing presented a systematic apologia of orthodoxy.
21. *A Discourse in Demonstration of the Apostolic Preaching*, v.
22. See also 4.7.4; 4,20,1; 3.24.2; 4.14.1. etc.
23. *Adversus haereses*, section IV.
24. Exod. 20.18 and 21.
25. Isa. 60.20.
26. Exod. 24.16–18.
27. . . . he did not know that the skin on his face was radiant after speaking

with Yahweh. And when Aaron and all the sons of Israel saw Moses, the skin on his face shone so much that they would not venture near him. But Moses called to them, and Aaron with all the leaders of the community came back to him; and he spoke to them. Then all the sons of Israel came closer, and he passed on to them all the orders that Yahweh had given him on the mountain of Sinai. And when Moses had finished speaking with him, he put a veil over his face. Whenever he went into Yahweh's presence to speak with him, Moses would remove the veil until he came out again. And when he came out, he would tell the sons of Israel what he had been ordered to pass on to them, and the sons of Israel would see the face of Moses radiant. Then Moses would put the veil back over his face until he returned to speak with Yahweh (Exod. 14.20–35).

[Jesus] took with him Peter and John and James and went up the mountain to pray. As he prayed, the aspect of his face was changed and his clothing became brilliant as lightning . . .
As he spoke, a cloud came and covered them with shadow; and when they went into the cloud the disciples were afraid. And a voice came from the cloud saying, 'This is my Son, the Chosen One. Listen to him.' And after the voice had spoken, Jesus was found alone (Luke 9.28–30, 34–35).

28. For other examples of the Shekinah see:
Exod. 40.34–35:

The cloud covered the Tent of Meeting and the glory of Yahweh filled the tabernacle. Moses could not enter the Tent of Meeting because of the cloud that rested on it and because of the glory of Yahweh that filled the tabernacle.

1 Kings 8.10–13:

Now when the priests came out of the sanctuary, the cloud filled the Temple of Yahweh, and because of the cloud the priests could no longer perform their duties: the glory of Yahweh filled Yahweh's Temple.
Then Solomon said:
Yahweh has chosen to dwell in the thick cloud.
Yes, I have built you a dwelling.
a place for you to live in for ever.

Num. 35.34:

You must not defile the land you inhabit, the land in which I live; for I, Yahweh, live among the sons of Israel.

Deut. 12.5:

You must seek Yahweh your God only in the place he himself will choose from among all your tribes, to set his name there and give it a home.

29. Exod. 33.9–11.
30. *Harvard Theological Review*, vol. 15, 1922.
31. A handful of French nouns can, in particular circumstances, be either masculine or feminine. For instance, 'an organ' is normally 'un orgue' (m), but if one entered a cathedral and heard the organ playing one might refer to 'les grandes orgues' (f). This feminine application of a masculine noun, generally in a rather literary context, would perhaps allow one, even in French, to refer to 'un espirit' when speaking of spirits in general, while reserving 'la Sainte Espirit' for the action of God in the Holy Spirit.

8 Who Is Our Holy Mother?

1. St Ildefonsus of Toledo (consecrated bishop in A.D. 667).
2. 1 Cor. 14.34 and 35.
3. 1 Tim. 2.13 and 14.
4. T. S. Eliot, 'Burnt Norton', in *Four Quartets*. See Eliot (1963).
5. 2 Cor. 3.17.
6. Cardinal L. J. Suenens, 'The relation that exists between the Holy Spirit and Mary', *The Way* (supplement), 'Mary and Ecumenism' no. 45, June 1982.
7. Elie Gibson, 'Mary and the Protestant Mind', *Review for Religious*, vol. 24, no. 3, May 1965.
8. ibid., p. 73.
9. Bulgakov (1937), p. 186 ff.
10. Latin: *columba*; Greek: *peristera*.

9 The Spirit of Freedom

1. John Donne, *Holy Sonnets*, XIV.
2. Ruether (1983), p. 69.
3. Rom. 8.1.
4. Rom. 8.21.
5. Isa. 11.6–8.
6. Acts 2.45.
7. Lauda lix.
8. Isa. 61.1.
9. Rom. 8.1.
10. Isa. 42.1.
11. 1 Sam. 11.6.
12. Judg. 14.5–6.
13. Judg. 14.19.
14. Acts 7.55–60.
15. Joel 3.1–3.
16. Gal. 5.1.
17. Gal. 5.13–14.
18. Julian of Norwich (1966), 68
19. Bishop Cosin, based on 'Veni, creator Spiritus'. *Hymns Ancient and Modern*, 157.
20. King (1984), p. 72.
21. Gal. 5.22–23.
22. Mark 10.17–22.
23. Luke 24.13–32.

10 Filled with the Spirit

1. Alexander Pope, *An Essay on Man*, II, 1.
2. John 3.8.
3. In terms of the wild-goose chase, it is perhaps significant that the wild goose used by the Iona Community is the Celtic symbol for the Holy Spirit.
4. Exod. 3.
5. Rom. 12.6 and 7.
6. 'When the Spirit of Truth comes he will lead you to the complete truth' (John 16.13); 'The Spirit is the truth' (1 John 5.6).

7. Matt. 12.12.
8. 1 Cor. 12.4–6.
9. 1 Cor. 12.29.
10. Acts 4.8.
11. Exod. 31.1–3.
12. 1 Cor. 12.9.
13. Acts 8.9–24.
14. 2 Cor. 3. 16–18.

11 Enfolded in Love

1. T. S. Eliot, 'Little Gidding', in Eliot (1963).
2. See Chapter 7.
3. Matt. 4.17.
4. G. M. Hopkins, 'God's Grandeur', in Hopkins (1960).
5. Acts 10.15.
6. See Taylor (1972).
7. Catechism, *Book of Common Prayer*.
8. This limit of seven was only arrived at during late medieval times. Hugh of St Victor, for example, who died in 1142, recognized thirty sacraments which he subdivided into three groups (*De Sacramentis Christianae Fidei*). Peter Lombard's *Sentences*, however, name the familiar seven (Book 4, dist. i, no. 2); and these were accepted by Thomas Aquinas and later affirmed by the Councils of Florence (1439), and Trent (1545–63). The categorization did not preclude other events and actions being recognized as *sacramental*, but restricted *sacraments* to particular channels of grace mediated through the Church.
9. de Caussade (1971).
10. 'The Blessed Virgin compared to the air we breathe', in Hopkins (1960).
11. A beautiful alternative Trinitarian Jesus Prayer has been composed by Fr Norman Goodacre, using 'Imma', the Aramaic word for mother, alongside the more familiar 'Abba':

  Abba, Imma,
  Holy Spirit,
  Jesus Christ,
  Eternal God,
  Have mercy.

12. Philosophers, from Plato to the present day, have frequently defined art and aesthetic experience in terms of the concept of contemplation. An analysis of this trend, and an exploration of the concept of contemplation in art and aesthetic awareness, was the subject of my PhD thesis (Surrey, 1983).
13. Heidegger (1971), p. 36.
14. 1 Cor. 12.13.
15. Matt. 5.48.
16. John 3.16.
17. *In Ep. Ioan.*, VIII. 12 (PL 35,2043).
18. Congar (1983), vol. 2, pp. 21–22.

Bibliography

All quotations from the Bible are either from the Authorized Version or, in the case of modern translations, the Jerusalem Bible.

A select library of Nicene and post-Nicene Fathers of the Church (W. B. Eerdmans Publishing Company, Michigan) Vol. IV, St ATHANASIUS, *Select Works and Letters*, trans. by Philip Schaff and Henry Wace, 1891, reprinted 1980. Vol. VIII, St BASIL, *Letters and Select Works*, trans. by Blomfield Jackson, 1894, reprinted 1968.

AUGUSTINE, *De Trinitate*, trans. by A. W. Haddan. Edinburgh, 1873.

BROCK, S. P. (1979), *Holy Spirit in the Syrian Baptismal Tradition*. The Syrian Churches Series, vol. 9, ed. by J. Vellian. Paderborn, Osstkirchendienst, 1979.

BULGAKOV, S. (1937), *The Wisdom of God* (a brief summary of Sophiology). London, Williams & Norgate.

de CAUSSADE, J.–P. (1971), *Self-Abandonment to Divine Providence*. London, Fontana.

CONGAR, Y. M. J. (1983), *I Believe in the Holy Spirit*, 3 vols, trans. by David Smith. London, Geoffrey Chapman.

CUMMINGS, E. E. (1963), *Selected Poems 1923–1958*. London, Penguin.

DOCTRINE COMMISSION OF THE CHURCH OF ENGLAND (1987), *We Believe in God*. London, Church House Publishing.

ELIOT, T. S. (1963), *Collected Poems, 1909–1962*. London, Faber & Faber.

FURLONG, M. (ed.) (1988), *Mirror to the Church*. London, SPCK.

HAYTER, M. (1987), *The New Eve in Christ*, London, SPCK.

HEIDEGGER, M. (1971), *Poetry, Language, Thought*, trans. by Albert Hofstadter. New York, Harper & Row.

HOPKINS, G. M. (1960), *Poems*. London, Vista Books.

JONES, C., WAINWRIGHT, G. and YARNOLD, E. (1986), *The Study of Spirituality*. London, SPCK.

JULIAN OF NORWICH (1966), *Revelations of Divine Love*, trans. by Clifton Wolters. Harmondsworth, Middx., Penguin Classics.

JUNG, C. G. (1969), *The Collected Works*, vol. 2, 2nd edn. London, Routledge & Kegan Paul.

KING, C. S. (1984), *The Words of Martin Luther King, Jr*. London, Robson Books.

LAMPE, G. W. H. (1977), 'God as Spirit', *The Bampton Lectures 1976*. Oxford, Clarendon Press.

MEYENDORFF, J. (1974), *Collected Essays*. Variorum Series.

MORLEY, J. and WARD, H. (eds) (1986), *Celebrating Women*. London, Wit and Mow.

MURDOCH, I. (1958), *The Bell*. London, Chatto & Windus.

PAGELS, E. (1982), *The Gnostic Gospels*. Harmondsworth, Middx., Pelican Books.

RUETHER, R. R. (1983), *Sexism and God-Talk*. London, SCM Press.

ROBINSON, H. W. (1982), *The Christian Experience of the Holy Spirit*. London, Nisbet.

STACPOOLE, A. (ed.) (1982), *Mary's Place in Christian Dialogue*. Slough, St Paul Publications.

SWEET, L. I. (1982), *New Life in the Spirit*. Philadelphia, Westminster Press.

TAYLOR, J. V. (1972), *The Go-Between God*. London, SCM Press.

VETTERLING-BRAGGIN, M. (ed.) (1977), *Feminism and Philosophy*. Littlefield, Adams & Co.

WHORF, B. L. (1956), *Language, Thought and Reality*. Mass., Massachusetts Institute of Technology.

WITTGENSTEIN, L. (1958), *Philosophical Investigations*. Oxford, Basil Blackwell.

YEATS, W. B. (1933), *Collected Poems*. London, Macmillan.